THE RECOVERY OF LIFE'S MEANING

Understanding Creation

and the Incarnation

THE RECOVERY OF

LIFE'S MEANING—

Understanding Creation
and the Incarnation

BY W. PAUL JONES

ASSISTANT PROFESSOR
DEPARTMENT OF RELIGION
PRINCETON UNIVERSITY

WITHDRAWN

ASSOCIATION PRESS, NEW YORK

Publisher's stock number: 1484
Library of Congress catalog card number: 63-10383

Printed in the United States of America

PREFACE

What is presently needed by layman, skeptic, and theologian alike is not so much new explorations into the complexities of particular religious issues, but the development of a creative synthesis of the insights of contemporary thought, centering in the interrelation between creation and the Christian message of redemption. The sources from which one must draw are no longer theological alone; they must include the insights of such diverse fields as literature, natural science, and philosophy.

At this stage, such an attempt means risking superficiality for the sake of generalization, attempting an impossible inclusiveness for the sake of a unified and overarching grasp of the whole. It is with such limitations painfully in mind that this present volume has been written.

There is much in what follows for which the writer is indebted. Those theological thinkers whose influence is most visible certainly include Nicolas Berdyaev, Paul Tillich, H. Richard Niebuhr, and Reinhold Niebuhr. Whatever value this synthesis and its original proposals may have, it is to be hoped minimally that its subject will be clearly exposed as a problem central to the understanding and living of our times.

I am indebted to the editors of *Theology Today* for permission to incorporate into Chapters 1 and 6 certain ideas and materials previously published there, to the *Journal of Religion* for like permission in regard to Chapter 2, and to *Religion in Life* in regard to Chapter 4.

To Association Press I am most grateful, not only for the invitation to write this volume, but for the willingness of its editors to support my firm belief that the general reader stands ready today to be addressed seriously in his own terms, and that such an invitation to dialogue in depth concerning the urgent problems of life and faith will find a ready response.

To my students at Princeton University and Bryn Mawr College, I owe my appreciation for the embarrassing questions without which thought and faith are impossible.

For the many hours of patience this book has caused my wife and daughters, I can only apologize; for their help in so many ways, for the joys given unrewarded, I dedicate this work in gratefulness.

I am grateful to Thomas Nelson and Sons and to the Division of Christian Education of the National Council of the Churches of Christ in America for permission to quote from the Revised Standard Version of the Holy Bible. All biblical quotations are from this version except where indicated (King James Version —KJV).

Acknowledgment is also made to the following publishers for their kind permission to quote from their publications:

Alec R. Allenson, Inc., and Dacre Press, A. & C. Black, Ltd., for quotation from *Finite and Infinite*, by Austin Farrer.

The Journal of Philosophy for quotation from "The Present Status of Natural Theology," by John E. Smith, Vol. LV, No. 22, October 23, 1958.

Alfred A. Knopf, Inc., for quotation from *The Plague*, by Albert Camus.

J. B. Lippincott for quotation from *Religion and the Modern Mind*, by W. T. Stace.

Macmillan Company for quotations from *Nature, Man and God*, by William Temple, and *New Essays in Philosophical Theology*, edited by Antony Flew and Alasdair MacIntyre (London: SCM Press, 1955).

New American Library for quotation from *The Limitations of Science*, by J. W. N. Sullivan.

Nisbet and Company, Ltd., for quotation from *Types of Modern Theology*, by H. R. Mackintosh.

Charles Scribner's Sons for quotations from *Farewell to Arms*, by Ernest Hemingway, and *The Christian in Philosophy*, by J. V. L. Casserly.

YMCA-Press, Paris, for quotation from *The Beginning and the End*, by Nicolas Berdyaev.

W. PAUL JONES

Princeton, New Jersey

CONTENTS

UNDERSTANDING
THE INCARNATION

INTRODUCTION

> For even as necessity, today and tomorrow, drives most men to think collectively in order that they may survive, necessity, day after tomorrow, will drive men to think personally (poetically, cosmically), in order that their survival may have meaning.
>
> —Waldo Frank, Introduction to
> *The Collected Poems of Hart Crane* [1]

NOT LONG AGO, the theologian regarded himself as possessing the ultimate answers to the question of the ultimate meaning of life, but more often than not they were answers to questions that no one was really asking. But our time is characterized by questions, with answers few. They are questions common to us all, for they are matters of life and death. Ours is a time that grooms neither arrogant atheist nor dogmatic believer. In our own ways, we are all searchers for meaning. And there is no hope for living answers unless the man of faith clarifies our questions, and the skeptic insists on clarity in the answers.

I am dissatisfied, as are so many others, with "popu-

[1] New York: Liveright Publishing Corporation, 1946.

lar religion," with the reduction of living faith to sentimental platitudes that neither challenge nor answer anything vital. I am dissatisfied, as are so many others, with "indifferent agnosticism," with the arrogant disregard for ultimate questions in which life and death come strangely to resemble each other. I am dissatisfied, as are so many others, with "irrelevant theology," with the polite substitution of German phrases for an agonizing wrestling with the common, practical issues of everyday thought and living.

Consequently, this book has three intents: to speak skeptically to the theologian, to speak theologically to the layman, to speak as a believer to the skeptic. This task is in no way a matter of "popularization," or of speaking "down" or "up" to anyone. It is a matter of beginning a desperately needed conversation in which the creative theological thinking of the present may be brought to everyday relevance, and the felt problems of the common, modern man may stimulate theological thinking to new understandings.

This writer makes no other demand on the reader than a serious desire to understand the desperate times in which we live and search, and to discover what dim outlines of ultimate meaning may be perceptible from this point in history.

Such matters as these are all implied by the subject of our considerations—Creation and the Incarnation. Although such traditional words seem so unexciting, so technically irrelevant for today's mind, contained in them are the very issues with which all of us are burdened and anxious.

Creation? Try the word on for size in this way—all this vast universe, and I but a speck lost somewhere within it; did it happen by chance, by blind laws, or have we any real basis for declaring with radiant faith, "In the beginning *God* created the heavens and the earth"? Or again, as I look at the star-spangled heavens, I sense a wisdom and a purpose that give peace and meaning to my daily living; and yet in that living I daily know the threat of anxiety, suffering, evil. I encounter the maimed, the exploited, the innocent child destroyed before he knows even his name. Under the pillar of fire that is no longer God's but the nuclear connivings of man, the so-called children of God become living Jobs, crying out, "O that I knew where I might find him."

And so to the Incarnation one turns, for here, it has been said, the God of love turned in suffering forgiveness to man, giving all that all might become new. Here is a vision, a promise, an answer that makes contact with the echoing need deep within each of us. And yet in the face of a creation that seems "red in tooth and claw," that seems indifferent or even hostile to our happiness, how can we believe in a God of love who is also the Creator? In fact, what could one even *mean* by the affirmation that "God became man"? Can black become white too, or squares also be circles? It is not really that one doubts such a statement, but can one say either "yes" or "no" to what seems to be nonsense?

How can another die for one's own sins—what could this possibly mean? Indeed, is the Christian also saying that the sins for which Christ died are mine and yet they were performed by the first man called Adam? And while we are at it, what about Adam? If evolution occurred over millions of years, how can you speak of Adam in terms of the sixth day?

Add to all this the insistence of the Church that the God who was in Christ is Trinitarian, and the response of our age seems unavoidable:

I come to you in anxiety, and you give me uncertainties.
I come without meaning, and you preach nonsense.
I come in confusion and you cry, "Miracle."
If my only choice is to be a Christian or a modern man, I have no choice. Modernity is my name—I am its child.

And yet, can man live if there is no ultimate meaning to life, if it is only "a tale told by an idiot, full of sound and fury, signifying nothing"?

These problems with which we must wrestle in this book, however, are far from restricted to the skeptic. They are clearly the problems as well of the man of faith, as faith inevitably seeks understanding.

These questions are at the heart of contemporary theology. It is a strange but fascinating fact that while

contemporary theologians are rediscovering the meaning and centrality of the Incarnation, they have been
led to this by the awareness that man's dilemma is
rooted in his alienation from creation.

Such a situation is quite illuminating to the history of
Christian thought. In periods in which creation has appeared harmonic and quietly assuring of man's success
in the mastery of man and nature, Christianity has become peripheral, the Incarnation regarded as needless
theologizing. On the other hand, in times in which
man's foe has appeared to be cosmic in nature, the Incarnation has been rediscovered, but at the cost of any
truly positive understanding of creation, of the material
universe.

The whole history of Christian thought can be perceptively seen as the attempt to unite in meaningful
dialogue faith in God the Creator with the revelation of
God as Incarnate Redeemer. If God be Creator, how
is it that creation stands in need of redemption; if God
be Redeemer, who then is Creator? So stated, it becomes clear that Christianity has never been able to
reach a clear verdict. The Church has never really
made up its mind finally about creation and consequently about culture. As a result, its witness has
fluctuated between the preaching of a supernatural
other-worldliness in which this world is a temptation
to be avoided, and a near humanism of culture-worship
in which God becomes unnecessary baggage.

This tension between creation and the Incarnation which haunts modern man is thus at its height in contemporary theology as well, posing an impasse for Christian thought. And yet it is at this precise theological moment that the possibilities for a creative resolution of the dilemma are arising. Among the fresh possibilities presently available are a radically new understanding of the scientific analysis of the universe, a Protestant theological renaissance for which the period of the Reformation is the only apt parallel, the development of such suggestive movements as "Theology of Culture" and "Biblical Theology," and the appearance of powerful works in contemporary literature in which the religious and artistic concerns are probed in their creative interrelationship.

The fact that these movements mean nothing to modern man is unforgivable. *The* question of our times is *the* question in contemporary theology; the resources available for a beginning theological resolution must be exposed in all their relevance through a dialogue with the layman and the skeptic.

For the sake of beginning such a dialogue, our approach in this book will be of this fashion. The task in Chapter 1, "Creation as the Twentieth-Century Enigma," will be to analyze our present times, aptly labeled the generation of crisis. What we must come to see is that our present dilemma stems from the bankruptcy of the modern optimistic faith in man and his inevitable progress. Creation, or the powers and structures of the world process, has seemed to turn upon man. Suffering, evil, death—these are the threats exposed to a generation that has known only war and the rumors of war. This is the situation that tempts a man to declare life to be meaningless; yet, without meaning, death becomes preferable to life. This is the human dilemma that we shall find posed so graphically in contemporary literature. It is the living awareness that creation is *the* problem of our times.

With such a posing of the problem, we shall consider in Chapter 2, "Creation and the Impact of Natural Science," whether a religious quest for ultimate meaning is even possible for modern man. It was natural science that not only stimulated our questionable faith in man's mastery of creation, but has tended to undermine the traditional affirmations of Christianity; yet we are the products of science and there can be no undoing of this fact. Our explorations will attempt to show how the maturing of both science and religion through our present conflict is freeing modern man from the narrow restrictions set by early science. The search for an ultimate meaning is not only possible but urgent.

In Chapter 3, "Creation and the Knowledge of God," our quest proper begins. We must determine whether God's existence can be proved. Through a consideration of the "proofs" we shall see how the

Christian doctrine of creation has been misunderstood through the past several centuries. Only then shall we be in a position to make the religious meaning of creation clear, showing how the existence of the Creator can be known without resort to special revelation.

With this beginning made, we shall see in Chapter 4, "Creation and the Search for Biblical Meaning," that this is only a beginning. What is the nature of the Creator? What of the problems of evil, of inhumanity, of human impotence, of guilt? Such problems as these we shall exhibit as those which drive the searcher for meaning to consider seriously the claims of Christian revelation. We shall consider how the truths of revelation, by their very nature, cannot be proved. Rather, what one must do is to come to understand the meaning of the Christian world-view by participating in it, coming to see it from within. Only in this way can the question of truth encounter a person.

Our concern from this point on will be to explore the Christian understanding of creation from the illuminating perspective of the Incarnation. In Chapter 5, "Creation for Covenant and for Incarnation," we shall see that this world-view begins with the portrait of every man painted under the title, "Adam." In the light of this understanding of man, we shall explore the biblical understanding of the purpose of creation and man's creative role within it. In terms of the risk involved in God's act of creation, we shall explore the presence of evil in the world as well as the nature of God's restoration of man to the creative task through Jesus Christ.

The intent of Chapter 6, "Incarnation and the Structure of Creation," will be to make the stumbling block of the Incarnation, the "God-man," intelligible to modern man. Finding our clue in the Covenant relationship ("copartnership") between God and man developed in Scripture, we shall attempt to understand the Incarnation in terms of the unity of Divine and human "wills." We shall find much suggestive help for such explorations in contemporary novels and drama.

Our next task will be to explore how Jesus Christ, as the fullness of the Creator God in man, illuminates man's task within an incomplete creation. By understanding God, we understand the nature of creativity and the Divine promise of eternal value to human creativity. It is in this light that meaning will be given to the idea of the kingdom of God as the goal of history and human effort.

In our last chapter, "Incarnation and the Transformation of Creation," such considerations will be brought to bear directly on the ultimate meaning of art and of culture. "Beauty" is the only category that we have to point to the fullness of creation that is the goal of God's plan. So understood, art becomes central in the understanding not only of man's nature but of the meaning of man within this world.

Such is a nod in the direction which I believe the searcher for ultimate meaning in our time must take. It is also, I believe, the path which the man of Christian faith in search of understanding must travel with him.

He is the image of the invisible God, the first-born of all creation; for in him all things were created, in heaven and on earth, visible and invisible . . . —all things were created through him and for him. He is before all things, and in him all things hold together. . . . For in him all the fullness of God was pleased to dwell, and through him to reconcile to himself all things, whether on earth or in heaven, making peace by the blood of his cross.

—Colossians 1:15-20

I ended up by finding sacred the disorder of my spirit.

—Rimbaud

CREATION AS THE TWENTIETH-CENTURY ENIGMA

O God! God!
How weary, stale, flat, and unprofitable
Seem to me all the uses of this world!
Fie on 't! ah fie! 'Tis an unweeded garden,
That grows to seed.
                    —*Hamlet*, I, ii

IT IS STARTLING how a seemingly commonplace idea can rest undisturbed in the corporate mind of a people for centuries, giving a quiet confidence to their vast activities, only to emerge one morning as no longer a self-evident truth but a haunting question that threatens one's life with utter confusion. The point of history in which we now live is such a morning.

Although many of us crave to believe otherwise, there can no longer be any doubt that ours is a generation of intense confusion, all the more so because all of us are haunted by questions more sensed than clearly discerned. Even in the arts, one can sense this with only one ear pealed to the atonal music of a Stravinsky, or one eye turned toward the tortured figures of a Picasso or the contorted sculptured forms of a Barlach.

It is in modern literature, however, that this inner turmoil at the heart of our times is most undeniable. Even the titles of our most significant works echo the cry of a profoundly disturbed people—Eliot's *The Waste Land* and *The Hollow Men*, Kafka's *The Trial*, Sartre's *No Exit* and *Nausea*, Faulkner's *Sound and Fury*, Camus' *The Plague*, and O'Neill's *Long Day's Journey into Night*. Here we sense a generation possessed, but no longer by the calm faith that once gave dignity and purpose to all life. We are a generation possessed by the specter of meaninglessness which will not be quieted.

How can one possibly understand this fantastic metamorphosis from the commonplace motto at the turn of the century—"Every day in every way we are getting better and better"—to the pronouncement of a Gertrude Stein several decades later—"You are all a lost generation"? The clue is in one of these commonplace ideas that has suddenly arisen from the death-by-familiarity to which it has been condemned, to become the molding question of our time. The only way in which we can come to understand ourselves is by seeing what few have seen, that it is the idea of *creation* that is at the heart of our contemporary dilemma.

"Creation"—the Nineteenth-Century Assumption

"In the beginning God created the heavens and the earth"—these words have a majesty about them that can give human activity an ultimate meaning. Yet this idea can be assimilated into other world-views that rob it of all meaning while still permitting it to convey a vague feeling of self-assurance. Such has been the case during the past several centuries.

For some time now, religion in general and Christianity in particular have been regarded as increasingly discredited by findings in diverse areas ranging from natural science and psychology to historical research and philosophy. But, despite this growing indifference to religion, something of the Judeo-Christian doctrine of creation has stubbornly persisted. Even in the nineteenth century, when human self-confidence rose to fantastic proportions and traditional Christianity was largely scorned, aspects of the doctrine of creation were not only retained but regarded as self-evident even in secular thought.

We see this in economics, for example, in Adam Smith's insistence upon "invisible" but unidentified "hands" which guaranteed harmony despite conflicting components of the economic scene. Even Karl Marx's militantly atheistic world-view rested firmly on a faith in the trustworthiness of the laws of the materialistic dialectic. Likewise, natural science founded its methodology on the assumption of the "uniformity of nature," on the belief that a *uni*verse was not a misnomer, that such "laws" as that of cause and effect were constant throughout space and time. Throughout this period remained the firm (but often undefined) faith in powers, laws, principles beyond human control that governed the universe for the profit of man.

To be sure, certain prophetic writers of the nineteenth century, such as Melville, Hawthorne, and Dostoevsky, warned of the demonic aspects of life that would not remain quieted, that would erupt violently to destroy those who take only a surface view of life. But to such warnings, the nineteenth and early twentieth centuries were largely deaf, worshiping instead their own capacities for infinite perfection and unending progress. The Christian doctrine of creation was used, ironically, to give men the courage that spurred the vaunted pride and belligerent self-confidence that made God irrelevant.

"Creation"—the Twentieth-Century Threat

In our own time, however, such warnings have become fact. This denuded but quietly assumed faith in "creation" is being shaken to the core. The very creation itself has suddenly turned in seeming vengeance upon an age that had taken it for granted. We are finally coming to know what Horace Walpole meant when several centuries ago he said, "The world is a comedy to those that think, a tragedy to those who feel." For an age that has known two world wars in one generation, the horror of a scorched Hiroshima, six million Jews burned in such gas chambers as Buchenwald, for an age going underground to face the future, the quiet assurance in creation that our fathers knew appears hopelessly naïve.

Natural science was the father of that nineteenth-century optimism, but now even among scientists a tremendous change in man's relation to creation is becoming evident. In the seventeenth century, Newton interpreted his scientific findings as proof of God's majestic act of creation, exhibiting the wisdom and purpose of the Divine plan. Creation was clearly on man's side. But with the emergence of evolutionary theory, for example, T. H. Huxley spoke for many in seeing in creation no longer a firm basis for theistic faith, but the contrary—an unearthing of the human dilemma.

Human progress, he insisted, is no longer the task of adoring creation and bringing culture into greater harmony with it. Evolutionary progress thus far has been the result of a ruthless and wasteful "survival of the fittest." But from this time forth, Huxley declared, the task to which we are called is *to remake creation, to effect a complete reversal of its very principle.* No longer can the human motto be survival of the fittest, but against "existence" itself "man must fight for the survival of the virtuous." Man must combat the amorality of the cosmos, protecting with human kindness the weak whom creation is intent on sacrificing.

LITERATURE AS A REFLECTION OF THE TWENTIETH-CENTURY DILEMMA

It is the creative artist who probes most deeply into the texture of an age and reveals its dilemma and possibilities. It is no surprise, then, that we find emerging as the central concern of contemporary literature this radically changed relation between man and creation.

Nineteenth-century literature reflected the vestiges of the Christian doctrine of creation characterizing that age. Whether such assumptions emerged in Whittier's "God is, and all is well," Browning's "God's in his heaven: All's right with the world," or a more secular version, it was inevitable that the chief human problem would be regarded as being primarily social. The title of one of James Farrell's novels sets the mood of this general nineteenth-century understanding—*The World I Never Made*. The problem was essentially that of the innocent individual, motivated by fundamental drives and needs which required social fulfillment, caught in an environment which thwarted real satisfaction. The problem was social, for *the* threat to man was a society intent on molding his total life. We see such an understanding in the work of such authors as Balzac, Dickens, Austen, Thackeray, Tolstoy, and Flaubert.

As this social understanding in literature was further explored, however, these writers and others began to sense mysterious depths in the human spirit. There emerged a growing premonition that the human dilemma rested finally in man's ignorance of himself. Although such writers still admitted that man discovered himself through social intercourse, it was seen increasingly that society, ironically, was a façade with which the self was veiled from itself. Here was the clue to the social dilemma—society threatened the self because the self was a threat to itself.

We see this brilliantly portrayed in the plays of the American playwright, Eugene O'Neill. Whether expressed through the dope-driven mother dancing with death in the silent upstairs in "Long Day's Journey into Night," or the whiskey soaks intoxicated in essence by their own pipe dreams in "The Iceman Cometh," the problem came down not to "the world I never made" but rather to "the self I never knew." It was the subconscious self that threatened man, erupting to destroy that which it could not dominate.

Yet the uniqueness of modern literature can be understood only in terms of one further step in man's understanding of the human situation. It is Ernest

Hemingway who stands as an important transition figure. No longer is man, social or individual, regarded as the real problem. Hemingway's "saved" characters are those who are sick of society, banding together in a code of simple pleasure and friendship. And yet, in *Farewell to Arms*, Hemingway makes clear the ultimate futility of even this. As the heroine dies in childbirth, she echoes the emerging awareness of our age— "It's just a dirty trick." The human problem has now been exposed, in the end, as cosmic, as transcending man himself. Hemingway's hero makes this unmistakable:

> That was what you did. You died. You did not know what it was about. You never had time to learn. They threw you in and told you the rules and the first time they caught you off base they killed you. . . . You could count on that. Stay around and they would kill you.[1]

The undefined "they" has now become the focus of the human dilemma. No longer is the problem primarily social, one that gives some hope of correction. Nor is it primarily a psychological problem, one that permits the possibility of therapy. The problem has its source not in man at all but in creation itself. Ultimately there is only a blind fate which crushes that which is indiscriminately given. *Man is cosmically forsaken. He is alone.*

[1] New York: Charles Scribner's Sons, 1953.

Beginning with this awareness, current authors have posed clearly the dilemma of our generation. Cosmic alienation is the cause of man's social and self-alienation. Only if man can come to terms with creation is there any hope of resolving the dilemma of self and society.

Albert Camus has expressed this for our time in a new myth, one intended to supplant that provided in Genesis. The biblical Eden surrounded by the concerned love of God has given way to a city walled in by plague. And what is plague? One character in *The Plague* makes it clear—"Just life, no more than that." Suffering, evil, death—these are no longer the product of the serpent. The plague which is life is no other than the work of the cosmic powers themselves, personal or impersonal, torturing and destroying the very life they create. André Malraux expresses this best: "You know as well as I do that life is meaningless; death is always there like a standing proof of the absurdity of life." Life is ended before we even know what it is.

Do you not now know beyond question, Camus seems to be asking, that Nietzsche spoke the truth—"God is dead"? Or, if we lack the courage to admit the obvious, must we not cry out in despair with Archibald MacLeish's *J. B.:* "God does not love; He is"? For a generation living under the threat of a nuclear holocaust, hearing the screams of human life which the offspring of Bach, Beethoven, and Brahms have symphonized in the gas chambers, or even for those who have known only the contorted face of a child eaten out by the patient thoroughness of disease—for these, Camus' own words cry out modern man's desperate plight: he is "fighting against creation as he found it."

Even if a God does somehow exist, "mightn't it be better for God," Camus asks, "if we refuse to believe in Him and struggle with all our might against death, without raising our eyes toward the heaven where He sits in silence?" What does this threat by creation make of life? Camus' answer is disturbingly clear—"a never ending defeat."

THE DEATH OF THE NEW "GODS"

The undercutting of the Christian world-view which has been occurring since the Renaissance, was first done with great jubilation. In his rebellion against the "shackles" of traditional religion, modern man first began to feel the intoxication of utter freedom. This liberation was not only from a dogmatic and dominating Church hierarchy, but increasingly from even a God who bounded life. Man was set free in a universe of infinite time and space, to bring all things to completion. Yet, more than these men realized, they had the comfort of the diluted Christian doctrine of creation or its vestiges to "guarantee" the meaning of their humanistic activity. This unbounded optimism marked not the death of God, but rather the substitution of new "gods" created in man's image.

The literary prophets of our time, however, are coming to see modern man's "liberation" in a far different light. Creation is no longer a comforting ally, but a ruthless opponent whose victories are never in question. For many, the old gods of religion have long been regarded as dead; but now the new gods of science, humanism, progress, and the like, have been shown by a seemingly demonic creation to be clearly unworthy of worship.

Viewing the modern situation, the historian Franklin Baumer has characterized us as "the age of longing," an age yearning for a faith that can liberate man from the threat of total meaninglessness that the question of creation has thrust upon us. Fear of death is not sufficient reason for creative living. The early exuberance over man's "cosmic liberation" has given way through the living of it to an awareness that such "freedom" is not to be worshiped; it is an oppressive burden, bordering on the nightmarish.

Jean Paul Sartre has stated this in a phrase: "man is condemned to be free." Indeed, what is invigorating in the vision of man as a speck of dust on the pebble that is the world, floating aimlessly and without purpose in an infinity of space in a time without beginning or end? Creation has finally humbled the man-God, and in our aloneness we feel a sense not of liberation but of cosmic isolation. It is to our time that the words of Pascal are becoming a living truth—"When I consider the brief span of my life, swallowed up in eternity past and to come, the little space that I occupy, lost in the immensity of space of which I know nothing and which knows nothing of me—I am terrified."

Camus' *Caligula* gives this awareness its modern form —"To lose one's life is no great matter. . . . But what's intolerable is to see one's life being drained of meaning, to be told there's no reason for existing. A man can't live without some reason for living."

THE CURSE OF SELF-DECEPTION

Despite the contemporary crisis, it is the ironic fact that ours is a time that is frantically veiling its eyes to keep from seeing. The demonic has shattered the optimistic faith of the West, but we refuse to recognize that this is so. As T. S. Eliot laments with a damning eye on our generation, "Human kind cannot bear very much reality." Or again, "We do not wish anything to happen. . . . We have lived quietly, succeeded in avoiding notice, living and partly living."

Life is being shaken to the core, but modern man shields himself with the remains of a once glittering tradition that has already been killed by the dry rot of commonplace familiarity. The demonic in creation has severed the cord of our self-sufficiency, but we continue to move to the same weary rhythm as before, willingly mesmerized by the fear of missing a step that will alienate us from mass conformity.

Staring out at the specter of a creation seemingly gone mad, Eliot screams to our times, "Do you know nothing? Do you see nothing? Do you remember nothing?" And as though in terrible reply, William Faulkner perceives the response of most in the portrait of a rotting family in a rotting house, shoring up the foundation with the refuse of empty tradition, as the termites continue their silent work. The things that matter most are at the mercy of things that matter least.

It is here that the significant writers of our time speak with one voice. All of them are obsessed with the symbol of "arrest," that moment of truth when a man is awakened from the stupor of inauthentic existence induced by the modern trinitarian deity of "material gain," "social status," and "temporal security." Only the man stripped naked by seeing his cosmic plight face to face is in truth a man. There may be no answer, but blind to the point of nonexistence is the creature who refuses to see the question of meaning that creation thrusts painfully upon him.

Franz Kafka speaks brilliantly for these writers, portraying our dilemma with the power of a parable. In

The Trial, Joseph K., leading the respectable life of a banker, is one morning "arrested" by mysterious persons for no apparent reason. In effect, his arrest is the dawning upon him of the ultimate question, "WHY?" When one is suddenly threatened by death or suffering or by any of the countless aspects of the demonic in life, he is sufficiently severed from mass conformity to be able to ask with ultimate concern, "What is the real meaning of life?"

Men are born, they live, they die, without any consciousness of existence, without ever raising in utter seriousness the only question ultimately worth raising, "*Who am I, and what ought I to do?*" We arise at the same time every morning, take the same bus with the same people to the same destination, doing the same job, eating the same lunch at the same restaurant, taking the same bus home, to sleep the same sleep in order to arise and repeat the same dreary routine over and over again, without thinking to cry out, "My God, WHY?"

We orient our split-level lives around money and success and popularity, and when even these leave us hollow and unsatisfied, we stifle our questions with an even more vigorous pursuit of these self-made gods. Those who cannot quiet the "why" questions, tend only to answer, "Why not?" But the greatest panacea of all is the New England excuse for everything: "Sir, this is the way that we've always done it."

As Eliot looked out at the "hollow men," the morning crowds moving silently over London bridge, he cried out in despair, "I had not thought death had undone so many." Without real meaning, life cannot be distinguished from death.

Why, why, why? This is the question that can turn a man's life into the nightmarish world of a Kafka. What is the meaning of life? Money? Promotion? Security? Social recognition? Is this meaning, is this life, when this too shall pass, when he who struggles and he who drifts both end with the same finality, when all the lofty dreams and ideals of man likewise end with him in the grave?

For Kafka, man is called into existence. And it follows that to be called is to be called by someone for something. But by whom is one called, and for what? Yet to be called into life by no one for nothing makes of existence a travesty. Life, meaning, truth, value—the contrary of all these is the one word—death. Man is called forth to live, but for what—to live for death? To quote Sartre, "My God, how funny." But this is the kind of humor that brings only tears.

Evil and suffering expose the same dilemma; for, as Tillich says, "Death is not simply the scissors that severs the thread of life, but is the thread woven into the very fabric of existence." Each day vitality is sapped from us, until death appears only as a halt to life's relentless unraveling.

The Religious Quality of the Present

In a real sense, this threat posed by an indifferent or evil creation is beginning to give a "religious" quality to our times. Such a quality, however, has nothing to do with any firmness of our religious convictions or piety. The religious quality of our generation comes rather from the penetrating seriousness of our questions. Despite our indifference, the question being forced upon us increasingly is *the* question of existence —"Who am I, and what ought I to do?" When asked with seriousness, this is *the* religious question, and every answer to it serves as a religion.

So understood, religion is universal. Despite the unacceptability or irrelevance that one might find in traditional, organized religions, no man can avoid making his own religious answer. Naked, man comes into a world he never made, nameless among the unnamed. There may be no certainties as he seeks to know himself and his place; and yet there is one certainty, the certainty that agnosticism is impossible. If a man had nothing to do but think, perhaps he could insist that ultimate things are unknowable. But to live is to act, and there is no act possible which does not presuppose some answer, one way or another, to the meaning, the value of life.

One cannot live without the assumption that life is preferable to death. One seeks that in life which makes it preferable, and it is his "god"; it gives to his life its basic complexion. Men have differed greatly as to the degree of consciousness involved in the religious dimension of their life. It is our generation that is being driven to a high degree of consciousness.

THE COMPLEXITY OF THE RELIGIOUS QUESTION

Not only is this ultimate issue being placed before our times with all its proper seriousness, but it is being exhibited in all its bewildering complexity. It is abundantly clear that there is no longer any easy or self-evident answer of any kind. On the one hand, the Christian must struggle to make his theistic confession in the face of the evil and indifferent aspects of creation, exposed as perhaps never before in history.

On the other hand, it is equally difficult to hold to atheism. Although the universe itself may seem to give no clear evidence of having any ultimate meaning, man nevertheless transcends this cosmos insofar as he experiences beauty, searches for and finds truth, raises the question of moral value. None of these things would seem possible if the creative "powers" that bring man forth are impersonal or malevolent. How can those qualities which alone give man dignity, that alone give him a meaning sufficient to continue living, exist in a universe that would seem to know man not?

If man had no capacity to understand, no ability to

reflect on himself and his universe, if he had no passion to love and be loved, if he had no awareness of human warmth and loyalty and courage, then death, suffering, and the silent universe would be no surprise. But man, knowing all these things, stands as a being that renders an impersonal creation an agonizing riddle.

The cosmos may have all the features of a deaf-mute, but if it is really so, why has man the frightful ability to turn to the laws of evolution and scream in despair—why have you made me so? Man so transcends the seemingly mechanical laws which have spawned him that life set eternally in the context of death stands as a living self-contradiction. *It cannot be, yet it is. It is, but it should not be. It should not be; then can it be?* This is the enigma posed by creation in our times.

Will Herberg states it well: "If there is no fulfillment more than human life or history can give, what is life but 'a tale told by an idiot, full of sound and fury, signifying nothing'?" [2]

THE FORCED OPTION

Among those who have been arrested by this question, there is a yearning, a questing for faith. And at the heart of this questing is a paradox that the non-

[2] *Judaism and Modern Man* (New York: Farrar, Straus and Young, 1951).

Christian thinkers have been unable to resolve. In periods when creation appears Godlike and man basks in the harmony of a universe seemingly permeated by Intelligence, man kills God with indifference; yet when creation appears to be void of Divine presence, it is only then that the religious question becomes meaningful.

We see this problem well through Camus' agnostic hero:

"Who taught you all this [about life], doctor?"
The reply came promptly:
"Suffering." [3]

That man must ever rebel against suffering, and yet obtain his dignity only through this suffering, is the mystery that Camus was never able to resolve. If the human task is to fight against creation, how is it, as Camus admits, that "it is in times of plague that there is more to admire in man than to despise"?

It is this enigma that drives one to explore with utter seriousness the Christian understanding of creation that we have lost.

* * *

How then shall we liken our times? Although the thinkers of a century ago would have chuckled at the

[3] Albert Camus, *The Plague* (New York: Alfred A. Knopf, Inc., 1948).

phrase, the questions being asked all around us today begin and end with the phrase, "the human dilemma." This crisis must be understood as the bankruptcy of the "faith" of the West. This faith is not the Judeo-Christian tradition, but a faith of man's own making, centering in a belief in inevitable progress, the unlimited perfectibility of man, and in the power of science to eliminate human suffering and need.

To such an optimistic faith, the events of the past several decades have come with shattering impact. No longer can we assume that creation, the "laws" and "forces" of the universe, are somehow tilted in our favor. We have seen evil, suffering, death, at first hand. And if these have the last word, where then is the meaning that makes life preferable to death?

We are at this moment trying feverishly to quiet such questions by a frantic activism, by so immersing ourselves in the "system" that there will be no time left to ask "why?" or "for what?" Yet in the silent, twilight moments, there is a hollowness that cannot long be forgotten. If we will not think, we cannot help but feel, and the feeling is one of anxiety.

Those who are arrested, those for whom such questions come to consciousness, experience the painful awareness that our problem is not simply a failure of nerve, a moment of misgiving that history will soon cure. This is the very arrest that has come to every honest man from the dawn of consciousness. This is not *our* dilemma—*it is the human situation.*

Although times of prosperity blind us to the fact, every man in every century, in every life—indeed, in every moment—is faced with the specter of death, with the shaking reality of human suffering, with the haunting possibility that all is ultimately meaningless.

There is the story of the dog who was being shipped by crate. To the dismay of a postmaster in a midwest office, the dog had chewed off the tag. Without recourse, the dog was sent to Washington with this note: "Here is nobody from nowhere going noplace." There is an analogy here to the human situation that is haunting.

G. K. Chesterton puts it this way:

We have all read in scientific books, and, indeed, in all romances about the man who has forgotten his name. This man walks about the streets and can see and appreciate everything; only he cannot remember who he is. Well, every man is that man in the story.[4]

Here, then, is the honest man: naked, in despair, threatened from within and without by a meaninglessness which undermines all reason for continuing. Talk then to us not of the irrelevance of the religious question. Say not that the question of God's existence is a purely academic matter. To our times, as it comes of

[4] *Orthodoxy* (New York: Dodd, Mead & Co., 1927).

age, the religious question is the only question which is ultimately worth raising.

Yet where is one to turn for answer when nothing is certain except our uncertainty?

CREATION
AND THE IMPACT
2 OF NATURAL SCIENCE

_____

> Man becomes a real problem to himself when as it
> were the original contract between the universe and
> man is dissolved and man finds himself a stranger
> and solitary in the world.
> —Martin Buber, "What Is Man?" [1]

THE FIRST STEP in our quest for meaning is clear. The
optimistic faith in man, history, and the cosmos which
creation is now placing under judgment was shaped
by natural science far more than by any other single
factor. We are molded so thoroughly by scientific
knowledge and its products that it is impossible for us
to reject science, even if we might wish. Consequently,
if we as modern men are to find any ultimate meaning
in life, the first step is to discover if, within the scientific understanding of creation, any such meaning is
even *possible.*

For centuries, science has been understood as largely

[1] Essay in *Between Man and Man* by Martin Buber (New York:
The Macmillan Company, 1948).

rendering impossible and irrelevant the Christian
world-view, except, as we have seen, for certain vestiges of the doctrine of creation. But today, as the inadequacies of the modern humanistic faith are being
exposed, scientists are beginning to take long second
looks at the supposed mortal victory of science over
traditional religion.

Re-examining the early scientific findings which
have been crucial in this supposed undermining of religion, W. T. Stace, in *Religion and the Modern Mind*,
raises the key questions:

> Surely God can as well exist with the earth going
> round the sun as with the sun going round the earth?
> Or is the existence of God consistent with circles, but
> not with ellipses? Or can he not exist in a universe
> which follows Galileo's law of motion, but only in one
> which follows Aristotle's? Finally, is the law of gravi-
> tation atheistic or incompatible with belief in a divine
> being? What then was there in the scientific revolution
> which could be inimical to religion? [2]

So posed, it becomes clear that the beginnings of the
infamous conflict between science and religion did not
really rest in any contradictory conclusions held by
each discipline. Rather, the real issue was the underlying assumptions of each. The thoroughgoing skepticism which resulted from seventeenth-century science
had its roots primarily in three places: deterioration in

[2] Philadelphia: J. B. Lippincott Co., 1952.

Western religious thought, the confident exclusiveness that science wrongly fostered about itself, and the unfounded arrogance of the Christian church.

DETERIORATION IN WESTERN RELIGIOUS THOUGHT

During this period of the rise of modern science, religion began to deteriorate to the status of an explanatory principle. Certain theologians in the Middle Ages, rediscovering the thought of Aristotle, had argued for God's existence by insisting that the existence of the world cannot be accounted for without a "First Cause," a "Prime Mover," and the like. Before long, such argumentation or "proof" encouraged the use of God as one uses the laws of gravity or of motion. God became a readily accessible principle of explanation for supplementing scientific theories at any point where they had been temporarily stymied. As we shall see, such Medieval theologians as St. Thomas Aquinas were insisting upon a kind of causality other than scientific causality, but this distinction was soon blurred.

Newton, for example, regarded his discoveries of natural laws, suggesting that the universe resembled a machine, as perfect proof of the existence of God. And yet he felt uneasy about his findings, for God was needed only to explain the origin of the system. Newton's religious faith was temporarily saved, however, for certain "errant" behavior in the way the

planets moved made it possible for Newton to bring
God in from time to time to save both God's system
and his own. The bankruptcy of this backhanded use
of God becomes apparent in Leibniz's observation that
Newton's God was simply a mechanic, and a poor one
at that, since He had to tinker with his own machine
to make it function properly.

The inevitable but disastrous consequence of this
understanding of religion was not long in coming. It
took only a century for Laplace to show that even
God's tinkering was unneeded, for these cosmic irregu-
larities were self-correcting. In fact, God was no longer
needed even to account for the origin of the system,
for the "nebular hypothesis" could account for the
origins of the world on a completely mechanistic basis.

Yet with the judgment on such misuse of religion so
imminent, the theist still tended to hold blindly to
God-the-explanatory-principle, obstinately raising the
question, "Who, then, created the nebula?" But when
this point had been reached, the devastation of theism
by seventeenth-century science was nearly complete.
Since God, for even the theologian, is by definition
ultimately unknowable, as He is in himself, God as an
explanatory hypothesis accounting for the beginning
of the world doesn't really explain anything. God becomes only an unknown "X" marking the temporary
limits of man's present understanding. As this understanding increases, in direct proportion our unknown

"X-God" disappears into the pre-cosmic mist. Laplace could not disprove God, but with the help of the theists he had done the next best thing—he had rendered God irrelevant.

Newtonian science had preserved God, but only in his remoteness. If God is to be more than an abstraction, he must be experienced as eternally present, as working immediately in all life. But science was pushing God back to the beginning of time, if, indeed, time had a beginning. Once God created the natural laws, they took over, and God had nothing further to do. If God's last act is to be dated in terms of billions of years ago, the existence or nonexistence of such a God is merely academic.

Once religion was understood as a way of explaining the existence and nature of the world, religion and science became rivals. The only resolution of this conflict seemed to be God-the-clockmaker, but with this deistic hypothesis, living religion died.

THE CONFIDENT EXCLUSIVENESS OF EARLY SCIENCE

Equally important in this period of the apparent undermining of religion was the self-understanding of the early scientists. With the first wave of success in the prediction and control of nature, the conclusion began to be drawn that the scientific laws and principles being discovered provided a complete explanation of the nature and thus meaning of all things. What at first were hypotheses became regarded as ironclad formulae. It is perhaps a natural feeling for one to think that he transcends something, is superior to it, in fact is in some way its controller and near maker, when he has described its operation in terms of mathematical formulae. These scientists believed that they had "reduced" the universe to its necessary laws, discovering the only manner in which things could function.

But here was the error, an oversight hidden by the vestiges of the Christian doctrine of creation. To say that things function in a particular manner is in no way identical with saying that they could not have been otherwise, or, indeed, that they will always operate as they presently do. On what possible grounds can one hold that the present "law" of gravity is the only way in which God could have created things? This is the same thing as asking how one could know that the law of gravity operates independently of God, that the law is because it "must" be. Indeed, if there is no God, if chance is the ultimate principle, what governs what can and cannot be? How can one talk of necessity at all? In everyday life, we know what "law" means, for there are lawgivers and law enforcers. But does the word have any meaning when extended to nature, if one denies a cosmic Lawgiver or Enforcer?

Such questions as these did not much concern the early scientists. They assumed that in the "laws" which they had discovered, the elemental foundation of all things had been reached, and the ultimate "necessity" upon which all things operated was exposed. As a result, God was useless.

It was the eighteenth-century empiricist David Hume who began to bring these troublesome questions to the fore. He saw clearly that there is no visible necessity in the way things work. When one says that an apple *must* fall, what can one possibly mean? All that one can mean is that it has done so in the past and *probably* will do so the next time. In saying that something operates according to a natural law, one is in no way accounting for what happens or showing why it could not operate equally well in some totally different fashion. He is simply giving a name to the orderliness that he sees. One vital question is certainly unanswered —WHY uniformity in the world? And if the scientist answers, "Because of natural law," he is redundant. Natural law *means* uniformity. To establish a formula for this uniformity is to show how the uniformity works in the sense of describing it; but that is all. The question of ultimate meaning, the question of why, still remains. The descriptive explanation of "how" and the requisite account of "why" are far from identical. But, for the early scientists, the only valid question was the descriptive question: and in their enthusiasm, they mistook the descriptive "how" for an answer to the question of the ultimate "why."

It was in this confusion of the two questions that the conflict of science and religion took its rise. It is only within the past generation, reflected early in such men as Sir Arthur Eddington, Sir James Jeans, J. W. N. Sullivan, and others, that scientific thinking is maturing to the point of perceiving that these are two quite different questions. The answer to one in no way provides an answer to the other. Further, scientists are coming to see that the scientific method, by its very nature, can deal only with the question of the descriptive "how." It stands for us to draw clearly the conclusion —none of the findings of science, in the past, present, or future, can ever decide the "why" question one way or another.

Science Versus Scientism

The insight that is emerging here is that it is not religion and science that are at war, nor can they ever be. It is religion and *scientism* that are at eternal odds. Scientism is the position which arbitrarily holds that the scientific method is the only proper method for understanding anything. The conclusion which is drawn is that all experiences and "truths" obtained in any other way are illusory or false. The scientific question is the only question, and any questions which science does not raise are illegitimate.

For a long period, scientism was regarded as synonymous with science. Contemporary scientists, however, are coming to see that the scientific method cannot be used to prove the exclusiveness of the scientific method without completely begging the question. The scientific method is one method for understanding one dimension or aspect of reality. Science deals with one question among a host of questions that man must ask in order to live. It is primarily the emergence of creation as an enigma that is forcing this awareness. Meaningful existence is dependent on a realm of truth and experience outside the descriptive scientific domain.

The Inadequacies of Scientism

There are a number of reasons for this early equating of science with scientism. In the first place, since scientific laws tended to be regarded not as hypotheses or probabilities but as necessities, all other methodologies, such as the religious, appeared anemic by comparison. If scientific truths were "objective" and "certain," it was not difficult to conclude that other fields were idle speculation, based on highly questionable assumptions. Today, however, it is clear that induction, the method of science, can never yield more than probability. No amount of observation can yield perfect certainty. Furthermore, science rests on fundamental assumptions (for example, the uniformity of nature, and the universality of cause and effect) which, in the nature of the case, are assumptions that cannot be proved.

In the second place, the early scientists tended to assume that reality was nothing more than the sum of its parts. Probably most of us have seen a plaster and wire model of an atom, complete with a nucleus and one or more orbits of electrons. In the earlier days of science, such a model was regarded as pictorially accurate. All reality was reduced to infinitesimal "balls" rotating at high speeds around a solid center. The whole was reduced to its least common denominator. Everything could be clearly understood by knowing these elemental and irreducible parts. Since all change could be explained by the redistribution of parts, there was no mystery left. All was clear, and there was neither room nor need for any other dimensions or perspectives beside the atomic.

Certain questions are being addressed to this point as well. To take an analogy from architecture, can one understand a Frank Lloyd Wright creation by reducing it to the building components of brick, steel, and glass, and the laws of engineering which hold these together as a whole? In this case there is clearly more in the work taken as a whole than can ever be seen through a microbe's view of the parts. How, then, could one ever prove that the microscopic view of reality is more true than the telescopic, or more valid than the view seen by the naked eye? It would seem to be more adequate to the facts to understand reality as composed of a plurality of dimensions or levels. Man's increasing observations seem to suggest a richness to reality that is destroyed by eliminating all other dimensions but one.

This one-dimensional understanding of reality which characterized early science is further questioned by recent discoveries that just as atoms can be redivided into sub-atomic parts, so even these can be subdivided until in the end what we get is pure, undifferentiated energy. As Eddington pointed out, what we arrive at in the end is not a solid model of self-explanatory particles to which all reality can be reduced. What we get are meter readings, and that to which the readings refer is beyond human powers of conception. That which the scientific method is capable of giving are the characteristics of energy measured in certain of its operations. What energy itself is, is a question that moves outside the province of science. By definition, such questions are beyond the capacity of the scientific method to answer. As Eddington states, "The chain of connection of the entities of the world is the province of science, but the intrinsic essence of these entities is now recognized to be outside its province."

It is at this point that the transition from the scientific to the religious question occurs. Such scientists as Jeans, Eddington, Pierre Teilhard de Chardin, and others, on arriving at this point, freely admit that they are passing from the domain of the scientist to that of the theologian or metaphysician. Yet, from where they stand, they see at the roots of reality, in energy or the depths of energy, that which resembles mind or spirit more than anything else. Although science cannot say, it could very well be, they suggest, that all things are what they are because they are thoughts in the mind of God.

Be that as it may, the end result is that scientific determinism can no longer stand unquestioned. In dealing with atomic structure, the scientific method explores only the surface of things, as it were. Beneath that surface, in the "thing-in-itself," at the interior limits of the scientific method, one finds a dimension of mystery that even the scientists are coming to insist is beyond the powers of the empirical method ever to know. It is here that the religious question of ultimate meaning again becomes real and must be met if it is to be resolved.

This point can be illustrated by considering the addition of electricity by modern science to Newton's list of "ultimates" (such as mass and force). As Sullivan observes, such an addition shows clearly that what earlier scientists had regarded as irreducibles that could explain everything might be far from complete. But even more important, in electricity we are dealing with something whose effects we know, but whose nature is unknown. The admission of electricity as an indispensable explanatory principle exhibits the fact that science need not know the nature of the entities it discusses, but only their mathematical structure. As Eddington and others insist, this is all that science can ever know, even of the Newtonian ultimates. In questions regarding the ultimate nature and meaning of reality, science must bow before a different discipline with a methodology designed to deal with such questions. This is the realm of religion; and the immediate point at issue, as we shall see, is the Christian doctrine of creation.

There is a third reason for the early identification of science with scientism. There is no question that the scientific methodology is exclusive in the sense that it is designed to deal with certain aspects of reality while neglecting others as irrelevant to its purposes. This is exactly as a methodology must be, for something cannot be understood unless it is set apart from other things for the sake of analysis. This is precisely what the early scientist did in establishing the scientific method. He singled out the quantitative aspects of reality for scrutiny. He was quite right in insisting that *as a scientist* the only dimension of reality that was legitimate was the quantitative one.

We are coming to see, however, that in doing this the scientist is in no sense saying that *as a man* the quantitative is the only legitimate sphere. Science insists only on a methodological exclusiveness. All that is demanded is that when using the scientific method one must regard all other considerations as irrelevant to scientific conclusions. Such an insistence is quite different from the claim that the quantitative is the only valid dimension of existence. If an individual wishes to go on and to make this methodological exclusiveness into a personal faith assertion about ultimate reality, he can certainly do so, but without the assistance or blessings of science. To take this radical faith step is scientism, a making of science into one's god. Scientism is something that science can never legitimately insist upon. It is a personal assumption whose validity can never be proved.

In the early days of science, however, this fact was not seen. We see this especially in the attitude of these scientists toward so-called secondary qualities. Primary qualities are the quantitative, measurable aspects of things, such as size, shape, and weight; secondary qualities include such characteristics as color, odor, sound, and taste. Instead of saying that the primary qualities were all that the scientist as scientist was interested in, these men insisted that the secondary qualities were not objective or real. They were discarded from the domain of the true for no better reason than that they could not be measured quantitatively. We are coming today to see the irrationality of disqualifying all qualities and experiences that do not fit conveniently into a particular method. Overlooking this, however, the early scientist placed the secondary qualities, and with them the truths and experiences of religion, into the limbo of illusion.

The New Self-Understanding of Modern Science

It was not the scientific method as such that rendered impossible the coexistence of science and the world of religious meaning. The conflict rested on the unfounded assumption that what was not disclosed by science could not be true. The change of attitude between earlier and modern science is radical, centering in this fact—the modern scientist now knows that it is impossible to legislate for nature. Experimentation is the final court of appeal. This means that the task of science is description. Earlier science, on the other hand, was an odd mixture of science and metaphysics, for by absolutizing the scientific method, a totally materialistic world-view was unavoidable. If the task of science is pure description in which one is ever the disciple of nature, following her ways by knowing that she is ever the master that leads, then science rests on no particular metaphysic, world-view, or "religion." Metaphysics or religion is a problem for the scientist as a man, not as a scientist. It is something that he must decide one way or the other for himself in order to live and be a man; it is not something that he must assume in order to get on with the scientific task.

We are prepared now to draw together the conclusions emerging from this recent scientific self-scrutinizing. In the first place, the scientific view of reality in terms of the smallest discernible quantitative parts must be understood as one method for understanding one dimension or level of reality. The attempt to convert the scientific method into an all-encompassing philosophy or "religion" is neither required for nor supported by the scientific method. That the whole can be perfectly understood through a knowledge of its parts can never be either a scientific assumption or a scientific conclusion. Whenever one says that science has disproved or replaced religion, he speaks not as a scientist, but as a "theologian" making the kind of statement which he himself condemns when made by rival believers.

Second, scientific knowledge is not so different in kind from other types of knowledge that one can regard it as intrinsically superior. Faith-assumptions are necessary for science, and scientific conclusions are hypotheses forever bereft of absolute certainty.

Third, science and religion are concerned with two different questions, the findings of each in no way undercutting the conclusions of the other. These different questions can be put in many ways, all pointing to the same crucial difference. Science is concerned

with fact, religion with value; science is concerned
with structure, religion with purpose; science is concerned with "how," religion with "why"; science is
concerned with actuality, religion with possibilities,
with goals; science deals with parts, religion with the
whole.

Fourth, science deals with the surface of things, not
because this is all there is, but because its methodology
requires a closed cycle in order to arrive at its metrical
conclusions.

The most significant change in modern scientific
thinking, then, a change with far-reaching consequences for the religious response to the enigma of
creation in our time, is the beginning rejection of the
scientific method as the exclusive way of acquiring
truth. If scientific truth is the only truth, man is an
accidental by-product of a huge, mindless, purposeless,
mathematical machine, duped by the illusions of meaning, virtue, and beauty, determined in his every action
to be an insignificant cog in an unending process that
is going nowhere. The cost of this faith-assumption of
scientism is high. Though in times of adolescent eager-
ness for freedom, the price was gladly paid, in times of
maturity created by the experiences characteristic of
the twentieth century, more than second thoughts are
called for. Unless it is absolutely necessary to assume
materialism, this is a step to be avoided at all costs. It is
one of the most important insights of our day, then,

that such an assumption is in no way required by science.

The Religious Implications of the "New Science"

This maturing of science is making possible a new liberation of the human spirit in its search for meaning. No longer can any experience of beauty, of virtue, of religious experience, and the like, be ruled out in *a priori* fashion. An understanding of man in all his fullness is again being made possible within the rich context of a creation with plural dimensions. No longer is science reducing life to insignificant parts. As Eddington has said, science "is now formulated in such a way as to make almost self-evident that it is a partial aspect of something wider." The emergence of the questions of religion through the enigma of creation, and the opening of new avenues for answers through the maturing of science, are providing the unique promise to our times for rediscovering a transforming meaning for human life and culture.

Though such meaning is not fact but a vision of new possibility that we must explore, it is in our generation that it will emerge, if at all. J. W. N. Sullivan's conclusion in *The Limitations of Science* states well this new and vitally important change in the present understanding of the relation of science and religion:

Our religious impulses cannot be satisfied with any-thing less than a belief that life has a transcendental significance. And it is precisely this belief that the old philosophy of science made impossible. We conclude, therefore, that the truly significant change in modern science is not to be found in its increased powers to aid man's progress, but in the change in its metaphysical foundations.[3]

THE UNFOUNDED ARROGANCE OF THE CHURCH

This maturing of science, however, is not the only important change in the opponents of the unfortunate science-religion controversy. Just as certainly as science stood guilty of overstepping the proper limits of its discipline, religion must be judged at fault, and for nearly the same reasons. During the Middle Ages, theology was known as the "queen of the sciences." Religious spokesmen proclaimed themselves not only as religious authorities but as dogmaticians in every realm of life and knowledge. The Bible was regarded not simply as a religious document but as the definitive textbook in natural science, astronomy, economics, politics, and the like. In fact, theologians came to so misunderstand their rightful domain that on the basis of Scripture, religious dogma, and tradition, they be-

[3] New York: New American Library, 1953. Permission granted by The Viking Press, Inc., copyright owners.

gan to dictate what could and could not be true in the total empirical realm.

It was this misunderstanding of the real nature of the religious realm that spurred scientists to regard their findings as somehow antireligious in nature. Overstepping its proper limits, it was inevitable that religion would be forced by the discoveries of science to assume an emotional defensiveness that confused the issues thoroughgoingly. As a result, these two types of truth came into conflict, each attempting to decide issues which belonged to the domain of the other, for which its methodology was not in the least equipped.

The Rediscovery of the Religious Issues

In such a situation, religion received one setback after another, setbacks that were quite often deserved. To a great extent, this conflict with science was fortunate, for it has been driving religion to take seriously once again those real questions which in its imperialism it had tended to overlook. At the very heart of this conflict was the question of creation, centering around the book of Genesis. Many theologians, seeing evolution as a threat to the heart of the Judeo-Christian tradition, felt obliged to defend unto death the literal account of creation in Genesis against increasing scientific evidence. This agonizing conflict which was responsible for much of the present dilemma could have been avoided had each side realized that the religious question is the question of ultimate meaning, the scientific question that of empirical description.

The religious import of the creation recital in Genesis is the affirmation that all things which come into being are continuously dependent upon the sustaining power of God, that the creative process is ultimately his doing, that the world was established by a Divine Purpose and that man is central in this design, that God is active in this history, and that all existence moves within the overarching intentions, principles, and limits established by God. But *how* God brought this world into being is a scientific, not a religious question. It is a question that must be decided by the scientific methodology. Naturally, the ancient Hebrews had their own primitive ideas of how the world came into being, and their religious assertions were inevitably couched in terms of this science of their day. This does not mean, however, that these religious affirmations must remain wrapped in a pre-scientific science any more than it means that modern science has any basis for judging the truth of these ancient religious affirmations.

THE PROBLEM OF EVOLUTION

All attempts to "reconcile" Genesis with evolution reflect a misunderstanding of the unique dimensions and questions which distinguish science and religion. Any similarity between Hebraic and modern science would expose an amazing Jewish ability for empirical observation, but in no way would either prove or disprove—in fact, in any way affect—their religious affirmations. When the religious man feels inclined to defend particular scientific tenets of ancient Israel, he cannot do this in the name of religion. He must speak as a scientist, and an incredibly bad one at that. The counterpart is the scientist who on the basis of science attempts to defend total materialism. In so doing he speaks not as a scientist, but as a philosopher or "theologian," and, to my mind, an incredibly bad one at that.

What science says concerning the process of evolution can be taken as valid, and the religious man can affirm without contradiction that cosmic history ultimately functions as it does because of Divine Purpose. For the Christian, behind each moment of the process of billions of years is God, in whose light man stands as the crown of an ultimate meaning that enwraps all time and all space. The explanation that evolution proceeds according to survival of the fittest, based on mutations, attempts to provide the descriptive "how." But why did "progressive" mutations without survival value occur coincident with others that did, being carried along until their survival value emerged? Why mutations at all, why these particular mutations, why any progressive mutations at all instead of only retro-

gressive ones? Why the emergence in man of those
abilities which give him his dignity, yet have no survival value, such as the love of beauty, truth, and good-
ness for their own sake? To these questions the
scientist as scientist must turn a deaf ear, not because
they are illegitimate questions but because they are not
questions that can be quantitatively decided. What the
scientist provides exclusively is an account of the way
in which evolution did occur. Mutation is not an account of why; it is a name for the fact.

Some scientists, if pushed by such questions, may
say that what happened happened because of chance,
but this dare not be taken as a scientific answer to a
religious question. In no conceivable way can the
scientist prove that there is nothing but chance behind
this incredible process. One can make such an answer
not as a scientist but as a religious man who is making
a personal decision about a religious issue.

In fact, if chance were a legitimate scientific conclusion here, it would indicate the bankruptcy of science.
Science is founded on the assumption that all things
have a cause. To conclude that the entire process that
brought all things into being was the product of
chance in whole and in all its parts is simply to admit
that most things have no cause and thus no explanation.
This science cannot admit. What we must see here and
explore later is that the type of causality involved in
the religious question is quite different in kind from

the causal pattern explored by the scientific methodology.

What if Science Succeeds in "Creating" Life?

One issue is appearing on the near horizon that could revive the religion-science controversy. What if science succeeds in "creating" life in a test tube? As in the case of evolution, such attempts in no way threaten to destroy the religious question with the scientific. What is required is a clarification of terms. The scientist is not trying to *create* life. His attempt is to reproduce those conditions in which certain laws of life can operate. We know that certain carbon arrangements are present in primitive life. Why that should be is not a scientific question; that it is so is the scientist's concern. He cannot create life, establish it according to his own laws. What he can attempt is to reproduce those conditions in which life does come into being according to its own laws. We do not command nature and succeed; we become her dutiful servant and she will respond uniformly and in good faith. Science seeks the principles of the world's operation, how they work, not what they mean. The ultimate mystery of life forever remains. The WHY of creation stands untouched by science, and man is called to form his own faith-answer in order to live.

SCIENCE AND MIRACLE

The same insights that we have already observed are beginning to appear in discussions of miracle. It is becoming clear that there are both the religious and the scientific dimensions in the issue of miracles, and that the scientific cannot undercut any meaning that might be revealed through the religious. This can be illustrated by considering one of the most difficult but central miracles of the Old Testament—the crossing of the Red Sea. It is important that we read the Exodus account: ". . . the Lord drove the sea back by a strong east wind all night, and made the sea dry land, and the waters were divided" (14:21). The scientific account of such a supposed happening would investigate the empirical conditions present (for example, the gale wind, abnormal tides, and the like), noting the various factors coalescing here to produce the event. Scientifically, one could account for how it all happened. Does this mean that God was not working here for the liberation of the Hebrews? Not at all. This further issue is the question of meaning, of whether chance or God was behind it all. This is a matter which science cannot decide one way or another, for whether it was God *or* chance, the scientific accounts would be identical.

This does not mean that what we have traditionally called miracle (namely, the "breaking" of a natural law) must be rejected in a scientific epoch. As we have seen, science formerly held that there was some sort of "necessity" behind natural law which, by definition, could not be violated. Modern science has abandoned such necessity. Natural laws are purely descriptive, and their hold on the future is only probable. A natural law is simply predictive, never legislative.

The "why" behind the orderliness of the world is a religious question. For the religious man, the "necessity" behind natural law is the orderly and trustworthy activity of God in sustaining and regulating life. Since such necessity rests in a Personality, it is not a necessity of blind conformity or consistency for its own sake. If the Creator God exists, the unity holding events together is a self-consistency of the Divine character in his purpose for men. If for the sake of God's purposes in the world, novelty, adaptation, and variety are required, there is no necessity within the scientific realm that God could be interpreted as "breaking." Natural laws are no more than human observations of regularity in nature, a regularity that is not more ultimate than God. Although miracle may be a variation from man's past observations, if the orderliness of the universe is a consistency of God's Will, both are expressions of the same order. They are made consistent by the consistency of God's over-all plan for the world. Consequently, whether one regards the world from the perspective of human consistency or in terms of

novelty made consistent by Divine goals, we are dealing not with scientific and religious incompatibles, but
with two perspectives emerging from two quite different questions.

* * *

We can begin to see now the fuller character of the
dilemma of our time. It centers in the lived awareness
of the enigma of creation, coupled with the haunting
feeling that science has ended once and for all the
ultimate meaning of creation to which the Christian
points.

We have not spoken yet, one way or another, about
the existence of God, nor attempted to defend any of
the other contentions of traditional religion. Rather,
our first step in the search for meaning has been to
establish one crucial point without which we can go
no further: science can in no way eliminate or decide
the religious issue. The questions of science and religion are quite different, and the method of one is irrelevant to the answers of the other. Science is an
important type of investigation that neither requires
nor defends any particular conclusion concerning the
meaning or meaninglessness of reality.

These limits which scientists themselves are beginning to place upon their discipline have been stimulated
by factors that are important to recognize. There is
not only a beginning awareness of the urgent need for

some religious answer to check the instruments of
destruction that have been created, but there is a
beginning feeling for the dimension of mystery at the
root of all existent things. It is this latter awareness
that is pointing significantly toward the real meaning
of the Christian understanding of creation, a meaning
that has tended for centuries to be lost.

3
CREATION AND
THE KNOWLEDGE OF GOD

> As long as man struggles only with the problems
> of his everyday existence—food, work, health, and
> sex—he is not very much above the animals; he begins
> to be a man only when he starts to wonder what life
> is all about.
> —Ignazio Silone, *The Seed Beneath the Snow* [1]

SINCE THE EMERGENCE of modern natural science in
the seventeenth century, the Christian doctrine of creation has been subject to misinterpretations and perversions until little of its real meaning has been preserved.
Only vestiges of it have remained in modern man's
understanding of the universe, until it is almost impossible for him even to sense what the Christian doctrine
of creation means. One cannot understand the Christian meaning of creation as an answer to the modern
dilemma until he understands these perversions and
sees how they have come about. One cannot simply
define what the Christian means by creation—it is a

---

[1] New York: Harper & Brothers, 1942.

unique way of looking at all that exists, and toward this
unique outlook we can only work our way slowly.

The key issue in understanding the Christian meaning of creation is the next step in our search for meaning—how can God be known?

A BIBLICAL POSING OF THE PROBLEM

In his Epistle to the Romans, Paul made a statement
that has posed for Christian thought ever since the
problem of creation and the knowledge of God.
Speaking of the atheists, Paul said:

> What can be known about God is plain to them, be-
> cause God has shown it to them. Ever since the crea-
> tion of the world his invisible nature, namely, his
> eternal power and deity, has been clearly perceived in
> the things that have been made. So they are without ex-
> cuse. (1:19-20)

Here is phrased the classical biblical insistence that
creation so witnesses to God's existence that man has
no excuse for denying him. The meaning of creation is
directly related to the question of whether the world is
so structured that it exhibits a meaning, a purpose, a
goal that is Divine. Is creation really a creation, the
work of a Creator, or is the creation a misnomer, a
random happening without design, purpose, or meaning? The development of the Christian understanding

of creation centered around this question of whether the creation itself witnesses to a Divine Creator.

PROOFS FOR THE EXISTENCE OF GOD

The question of the knowledge of God through creation has centered, especially since the Middle Ages, in the matter of the "proofs" for God. The first real attempt to relate the Christian understanding of creation with the new Aristotelian empiricism that prefaced modern science occurred largely through the thought of St. Thomas Aquinas. St. Thomas brought together five arguments for God. His first argument will serve well to help us discover the Christian understanding of creation to which he was pointing; it will serve as well to indicate the perversions that occur when this understanding is made into a proof.

By looking around us, he began, we can easily see that many things are moved, that is, they have potentialities which become actual. It follows, he continued, that something which is only potential cannot actualize itself. For example, an iron bar has a potentiality for hotness, but it will become hot only when something which is hot comes in contact with it. Now in order to account for such motion, St. Thomas argued, sooner or later we must affirm a First Mover. We cannot keep going through an infinite series of movers or we shall be unable to explain anything. Without an

Unmoved Mover, motion is impossible. This First or Unmoved Mover "all men call God."

This way of arguing is the basis for what has been traditionally called "the cosmological argument." It is the attempt to infer what is required by the existence of the world. Empirical reality, the argument goes, by its very nature, requires a Creator. Though such arguments had some success in the Middle Ages, they have since been undercut not only by philosophy, but, as we have indicated, by advances in science. The heart of the critique is this. On what basis can one insist that an infinite series of movers or causes is impossible? Newton, for example, established the law whereby an object in motion remains in uniform motion "except in so far as it may be compelled by an external force to change that state." On the basis of this law, it could well be maintained that the cosmic process has been eternally in motion, therefore not requiring a First Cause.

What is most important about this critique, however, is that it shows how thoroughly the age of early science misunderstood the idea of creation to which such arguments were pointing. The argument was interpreted as though with the analogy of dominoes in mind. Probably all children have set dominoes on their ends, close to each other in a line, pushed the first domino, and watched each push over the next until the motion has run through the entire series.

With such an analogy in mind, it was natural to suppose that what such men as St. Thomas were after was, as it were, a first cosmic domino pusher. Consequently, even if one were willing to admit the need for such a Being, the result was only an innocuous deism in which God's only action was at the beginning of time. With one flick of the finger, in effect, God became irrelevant to everything which followed. The doctrine of creation, so understood, was an irrelevancy, even *if* true.

Creation as Dependency

This, however, was *not* what St. Thomas had in mind. Although his words seem at points to support such an interpretation, he himself maintained that it is impossible ever to prove that the world has not always existed. In other words, one cannot prove that creation had a beginning. It is clear, then, that St. Thomas was not maintaining that an infinite horizontal series of movers stretching infinitely into the past is an impossibility. What, then, could such an argument mean?

Although the Christian idea of creation that St. Thomas had in mind is difficult to grasp, let alone prove, the meaning is understandable if we distinguish between a "horizontal series" and a "vertical series." This idea is so central for our understanding of creation that I beg the reader's special attention as we try to make this clear.

Suppose that the world has always existed. Then we would have an infinite horizontal series in the sense that whenever we asked what moved a certain thing we would point to something in the past which itself was moved by something earlier, and so on. There would be no reason to stop pushing further into the past. If we got tired and gave up by saying that God was the First Mover, we might quite rightly be asked, "Who made God?" Such explorations get us nowhere in solving religious problems because we are in the realm of science here. How things came to be is the question that is really being dealt with in the horizontal series, and the astrophysicist and his colleagues have the last word.

Now let's look at such matters in a different way. Even though the world process might have had no beginning, this in no way changes the fact that it is composed of dependent (or what has been called "contingent") things. Since everything in the series is contingent, there is no necessity in the series, no reason that the series couldn't have been radically different than it is. This is the fact, as we saw in the previous chapter, that Hume and modern science have seen. All we can say is that the world is, not that it must be. Even though the world process might be infinite in time, there is nothing in it that requires it or anything to exist at all. There is nothing in the series for which nonexistence would be self-contradictory. It is quite possible to imagine that sometime nothing will be.

Now since the series is in no way necessary, the series cannot explain or account for itself. By saying this, we do not mean that the series needed something or someone to start it. What we do mean is that neither the world nor anything in the world can account for the fact that anything exists at all, or for the fact that anything that exists should continue to exist in this moment, and the next, and the next.

An illustration would no doubt be appreciated here. An example of horizontal dependence would be the dependence that a child has on its parents for its birth. Vertical dependence, the continuous dependence of the *total* series on something outside itself, is the kind of dependence that a lamp has on the sustaining power of the electrical current in every moment. The fact that the child is horizontally dependent on something outside itself only points to the fact that every member of the series is dependent—the series as a whole is dependent.

In terms of the world process, vertical dependence means that all things that exist and have existed are dependent in every moment for their existence and operation on "laws" that hold them together as a temporal series. To account for such "laws," in fact to give the word any meaning, one must ascend vertically in explanation. The question here is not how did something come into being (for example, because of its parents), but why does it exist right now, what sustains it, why (like the light) does it not disappear? Everything continues to exist because it is undergirded by a uniformity and consistency that, as modern science says, cannot be accounted for either in terms of the objects themselves or in terms of descriptive natural laws. The end of our vertical reasoning brings us to a Being who is not himself dependent; either we affirm the existence of this Being or we cannot affirm the existence of anything in this moment.

When one talks about horizontal causes, raises the question of "how," he can keep pushing the question back into the past, and by assuming unlimited time, can escape the question of a First Cause entirely. But when one speaks of vertical causality, time is not involved at all. The question, the religious question, is this: what in *this* moment is supporting the series and the laws of the series by which one thing changes its characteristics with uniformity and other things come into being with perfect regularity? Or to get at it at its deepest level: why something rather than nothing? One cannot push this question back into the past; it has to be pushed into another dimension of being, as it were, into a transcendental sphere, to a type of Being that is necessary, that needs no explanation except its own nature. If the vertical series does not end at some point, then one is in the impossible position of being unable to account for existence, motion, or causality at all, for it has no foundation. Either there is an undergirding Ultimate Cause of all things in each moment, or one is forced to the impossible position of denying all motion, all material causality, indeed, all existence. What the cosmological argument insists is that by a consideration of temporal existence one is pushed into the religious realm of Ultimate Causality, to a Cause which is not *once* in time (at the beginning), but a Cause that undergirds the whole series in every moment and in every aspect of its operation. This is the central point of the Christian understanding of creation, and not, as is generally assumed, whether or not the world had a beginning. By First Cause or Mover, then, is meant Ultimate Cause, not original cause.

The difficulty with such "proof" is that although it is almost self-evident to the Christian that all things are created, that is, are radically dependent upon God, such contingency is anything but obvious to the nonbeliever. In fact, it is almost beyond the nonbeliever to imagine what else besides horizontal causality one can possibly be talking about. Consequently, it seems to the nonbeliever that scientism is the perfect answer to the only type of question that he sees. When Bishop Butler expressed fascination over the fact that a stone observed outside his study one evening was there in the morning, it is not to be wondered that some of his

secular friends feared for the good Bishop's health.
This awareness of vertical contingency is not something that can be logically proved. It is something
which the argument assumes. Such an argument is, as
we shall see, a valid description of a felt awareness,
what could be called an intuition, but it is in no way a
rational proof or demonstration.

PROTESTANTISM AND THE PROOFS

The new situation emerging in our time is promising
in terms of the issue before us. The convergence of the
new understanding of science with the enigma of creation is creating a unique situation in which the living
truth of the Christian doctrine of creation may be discovered. This doctrine, as we have seen, is not an explanatory principle for answering the "how" of the
cosmic process. Its concern is with an ultimate meaning that transforms man's existence with purpose by
answering the question of "why."

To understand this opportunity presented by our
present crisis, we must consider two types of criticism
brought against the Thomistic type of argument. The
first was provided by traditional Protestantism. For
Calvin, man's basic problem was not "how can God be
known?" The crucial problem centered on man's condition. Only knowledge of a very special kind could
answer the human dilemma. Man's predicament is the

self-centeredness of each individual, his utter worship of self. Consequently, man's failure to believe in God is not a matter of ignorance but of will, of choice. What man needs is not proof but redemption, a shaking and reorientation of his very personality. Even if a perfect proof were possible, it would be ineffective as long as a man loves himself with "all his heart, and mind, and soul, and strength." Man wills to be supreme, to acknowledge dependence upon no one but himself. *He craves to be god.*

For Calvin, the problem of knowing God is this: man does not *want* to believe, *despite* the evidence. As long as the question of belief in God is not a matter of evidence (which Calvin sees abundantly in creation) but of a twisted psyche that refuses to sacrifice its idolatry of self, family, or nation, the "proofs" are irrelevant and misdirected.

I am reminded of a student magician that I once saw at a Princeton party. He had two persons place their hands on four sides of a black box, and he put his hands on the remaining two. At the count of three, that black box disappeared. And although I saw it disappear, and it can be attested to by seventy-five Princeton professors, do you think that I really believe that there is a student on this campus who can make little black boxes disappear? Of course not, because I do not wish to believe it. What would happen to my world if it were true? And what is more, there is nothing that that student could ever do to convince me otherwise. It is not a matter of evidence; it is a matter of will.

MODERN PHILOSOPHY AND THE PROOFS

The second critique which we must understand in our search for meaning is that provided by modern philosophy. Beginning with René Descartes (1596-1650), the problem which obsessed philosophers was this: how can we know anything with certainty? Whatever we try to know is always separated from us. I am a subject; it is an object. It is this separation which deceives us into seeing things that are not so, as, for example, when we see an oar in the water that appears bent. How, then, can we distinguish with certainty truth from deception?

It was the German philosopher Immanuel Kant (1724-1804) whose answer has set the tone of modern philosophy. We can have objective knowledge of the world, he insisted, but not in the old sense. All men perceive a particular object in the same way, not necessarily because this is the way that the object is in itself, but because man's mind is so structured that he has no alternative. The mind organizes all sense data according to its own laws or categories. One such category is that of cause and effect: men cannot help seeing everything according to a causal pattern.

It is here that the problem enters. Since science deals with the relations between empirical things as seen from the human perspective, scientific knowledge is possible; since religion, however, is concerned with the innermost essence or meaning of things, with things as they are in themselves, religious knowledge is impossible. St. Thomas was right in insisting that all things have a cause, but this is only because the human mind is so made that it cannot perceive things in any other way. The only kind of causality that the mind requires in perceiving the world, moreover, is horizontal causality. This is the realm of the scientific "how."

Kant rightly saw that when one inquires about a vertical First Cause, he is really asking whether the innermost nature of things is such that it is self-sustained in every moment, requiring no sustaining God, or whether all things in the core of their existence are radically dependent upon a Creator who undergirds them and the entire causal series in every moment. To put this in Kant's terms, scientific knowledge is restricted to *phenomena*, to the surface of things as they appear to man. The *noumenal* dimension, however, things as they truly are in themselves, is closed to rational certainty. Consequently, despite St. Thomas, a vertical or religious First Cause is not *logically* required; the "proofs" prove nothing.

To summarize the central criticisms of the proofs, classical Protestantism insists that even if rational knowledge of God were possible, man is such that he will not accept it; the philosopher insists that such rational knowledge of God is not even possible. From one perspective, this twofold attack upon the traditional proofs can be seen as partly responsible for the rejection of theism in general and Christianity in particular. Viewed from another perspective, however, such critiques must be seen as attacks against the perversion of the Christian doctrine of creation. They have helped to clear the debris so that something of the real meaning of the Christian doctrine of creation can begin to be seen. As we shall try to make clear, the issue is not that creation fails to give any awareness of God's existence, but that Thomists and others are mistaken in holding that such knowledge can and should be acquired by logic, by rational proof. All such attempts are impossible, ineffective, and even more important, thoroughgoingly misleading.

PERSPECTIVES AND DIMENSIONS OF REALITY

Kant's insistence upon a noumenal dimension of existence inaccessible to observation is the philosophical underscoring of the new scientific awareness that the scientific method cannot provide the total knowledge of existence. This awareness is the first step in reopening the religious question.

But Kant did far more than reopen the question; he

provided a fresh approach for finding an answer. Though rational knowledge of God is impossible, Kant came to see that in moral experience and in the experience of beauty one obtained sufficient grounds for theistic *faith*. There is much disagreement over the validity of Kant's conclusions here, but his conclusions were not the important thing. His ideas stimulated Protestant thinkers and others to see that there is a plurality of legitimate human experiences with what can be called corresponding dimensions of being. It is to a clarification of this awareness that we turn for the next step in our search for ultimate meaning.

Kant pointed to the dimensions of reality in several ways. In the first place, in distinguishing between the phenomenal and noumenal "realms," Kant was recognizing the existence of other dimensions to things besides the purely empirical, common-sense plane. Reality is composed of different dimensions which together compose reality and every object in it. One has an anemic view of existence if it is experienced only in terms of one perspective and understood one-dimensionally.

Second, reason and empirical perception are not the only human faculties with which to perceive reality. In defending both aesthetic perception and moral experience as legitimate, Kant was exhibiting a number of human capacities for experiencing various dimensions of reality, each revealing not rival understandings but complementary, equally valid aspects of reality. Although for the Christian, as we shall see, this opening of the fullness of creation is based, at least in part, on the revelation in Christ, it is important that we see this richness being underscored by such recent developments in other realms of human exploration.

The meaning of this idea of dimensions of reality can be best shown by means of an illustration. Let us consider, for example, a Botticelli Madonna. On the one hand, such a painting can be investigated scientifically; one can analyze the pigmentation for its own sake, or as a clue to the problem of dating, or as the basis for discovering new possibilities in the mixing and blending of color. Or one can regard it artistically, studying it as a problem in form and symmetry, as a problem in composition, perspective, or technique. Still further, it can be studied historically, in terms of the schools of painting that influenced Botticelli, the history of the symbols used, or the degree to which this painting reflects the times in which it was created. Or it can be looked at theologically, analyzing the understandings of Incarnation, Virginity, and Divinity which are being portrayed.

On the other hand, one can leave all these "objective" analyses behind, and enter into the work of art as a whole. That is, one can enter into an aesthetic experience with the work, becoming so entranced by its beauty that he is raised out of himself and made one with the transformed world of Botticelli's creation. Or, still again, one can enter into a religious experience through the work, participating in it as an object of religious devotion, as a symbol of one's ultimate faith, as Botticelli must have meant the work to be taken.

What becomes clear here is that no one of these perspectives taken in isolation gives us the Botticelli painting. The work is all of them and more, taken as a whole. None of them are mutually exclusive, and the work is anemic if limited to any one or several. This illustration is analogous to the kind of understanding which certain philosophy and the maturing of science are beginning to suggest.

THE UNIVERSALITY OF THE RELIGIOUS PERSPECTIVE

Correlatively, the enigma of creation is beginning to force the awareness that the religious is one of these unavoidable perspectives. Kant said that the categories of the mind make it subjectively necessary for man to understand things in certain ways. But is it not likewise true that man is so structured that he requires meaning in order to remain in existence? Every man, whether he is conscious of the fact or not, has an object of supreme devotion from which his meaning for living is derived. Religion is best defined not so much by the object to which one is supremely related as by the kind of relationship that is involved. One can be religious in his relation to sex, money, country, or self, if one or a pantheon of these is the object of his ultimate concern, if his life-meaning is derived through this orienting dedication. Man, of necessity, is religious. The central religious question, then, is not whether or not one should "believe," whether or not one should have a faith-orientation or ultimate commitment. Man, by his very nature, has no option. The question is, *which* faith is reliable in the living of it; which "god" gives the fullest meaning that existence can support?

What becomes clear here is that the kind of religious orientation which is subjectively necessary for man as man is not the kind that can be derived through "proofs," through rational conclusions. Religion is not a matter of what a man says he believes. It is not belief at all, but faith. It is one's total orientation, a matter of *lived meaning*. It is not simply the commitment of one's rational faculties, but the relation of the whole man to something. With real insight Kierkegaard once stated that a pagan involved with his wooden idols with infinite passion is far more religious than the passionless Christian with all the correct beliefs. Man is at his best when he worships that which he finds greatest.

THE RELIGIOUS DIMENSION

But even if one cannot escape being religiously oriented to some object, can one avoid the conclusion that every choice is only subjective? Is there an experience possible whereby man can enter into relation with a unique religious dimension of reality itself that can make a claim to be objective? This is to ask if the Christian insistence that all things in existence are by nature radically dependent is a religious answer that can be known by every man. The "proofs" failed to provide any objective answer to the religious question; yet is the understanding of creation to which the "proofs" point, the religious dimension of contingency in all things, available in some other way than through logic?

It is as though in answer that the enigma of creation in our time is opening up such a possibility, a possibility that was particularly difficult to recognize in other periods of history. Calvin was perceptive indeed in insisting that the religious problem is not evidence for God, but man's unwillingness to admit any higher Being to whom he owes allegiance. Without a living awareness of the *need* for God, the question of God's existence becomes only an academic matter in which the philosophically inclined can dabble.

But the enigma of creation, encountered personally, can shatter man's self-sufficiency, his vaunted arro-

gance, and thrust the total man into the agonizing
search for meaning. Only the total man, as an acting,
willing, feeling, fearing, threatened, despairing creature, can ask the meaning of existence with the religious seriousness sufficient to find answer. In our
cultural situation, we are seeing far more than a desperate historical situation for which God might be a
convenient escape mechanism. This situation exposes
in his nakedness not simply modern man, but man as
such. As T. S. Eliot has said through our age to every
age, "Come and I will show you fear in a handful of
dust." Men need not wait until the walls of civilization
tumble before knowing the human dilemma which is
ours if man is supreme, although such tumbling is necessary to awaken most. In a handful of dust we see all
that will remain of any of us. Here is man existentially
involved in the religious question—standing naked,
threatened from within and without by a meaninglessness which undermines all reason for continuing.

The Leap of Faith

Some existentialist Christians maintain that the only
"knowledge" of God to be gained is through the
"wager" which the enigma of creation forces man to
make. Since no answer to the ultimate question is certain, man is forced, as Tolstoi once insisted, to affirm
God or die.

Yet there is a problem here. Can one really believe with all his heart, mind, soul, and strength, that God exists, if all that the enigma of creation thrusts upon him is the overwhelming wish that it be so? We are told that man has no choice but belief in God or despair. If this is the only choice, in the name of honesty I, with Sartre, must choose despair. Such an approach to the problem of ultimate meaning appears to be not a "leap of faith" to God but a "leap from despair" toward a fond hope. The charge of escapism here is not without point.

The Act of Introspection

But there is another possibility in the search for ultimate meaning. It begins with the recognition that the religious question concerns the noumenal dimension of all things. The religious question is this: at the heart of existent things is there self-sustaining matter, that which is its own explanation, or by its very nature is it forever God-dependent in order to be?

Philosophers and scientists are beginning to see, rightly, that both logic and the scientific method are barred from answering this question. But if there is one case in which phenomenon and noumenon are identical, in which subject and object are one, then the chasm between knower and known that destroys certainty would be overcome. Only then would the truth about reality, the ultimate meaning, if any, be exposed.

This is just another way of asking, "What is it like to exist?" It is obvious that a man can never become a tree or flower, can never know these from within, experience their noumenal essence, discover what it means for them to exist. This becomes even more clear when one considers the impossibility of ever truly knowing another person. No matter how much one may live with another, there is always a mysterious center, the other self, that remains hidden behind the outer actions that we see and on which we make our guesses. Yet what the Thomists and other advocates of the cosmological arguments were attempting to do was to arrive at certain knowledge of God through external objects. Of such external objects, however, man is ultimately ignorant. Such objects are destined to remain objects which confront man, always at a distance.

What, however, about the case of the introspective self? Is this not the key for which we are looking? Here is the one case in which the subject, the apprehending self, is identical with that which is being apprehended, likewise the self. Here subject and object are identical. If man is ever to know the "really real," the "truly true," that innermost depth of reality that scientists such as Eddington clearly recognize but see as forever beyond the grasp of scientific investigation, it will be in the process of the self introspecting profoundly the depths of its own existence.

And what does man see as he peers into his own depths? This is the question on which man's total life depends, for it is only here that he can finally settle for himself the question of God or chance.

The Experience of Contingency

In putting the search for religious meaning in this way, we are placing ourselves within a long tradition in Christianity for understanding creation, that emerging in Augustine, continuing through the medieval Franciscans, and entering into contemporary Protestant thought through such men as Friedrich Schleiermacher (1768-1834). J. V. L. Casserley's summary of Augustine's understanding provides the insight for which our age is keyed:

> [Augustine] begins with the indubitable fact of self-consciousness. . . . Such self-knowledge is unique because it is knowledge from within. All other things are known from without, and the possibility of total error cannot be excluded without careful thought and discussion, but self-knowledge is different in kind from all other types of knowledge. . . . But, and here we come to the essence of Augustine's theism, this immediate self-consciousness is not a consciousness of the self alone. I know that I am, but at the same time I know that once I was not. The being which I know in my self-consciousness is clearly not an independent, self-explanatory being. My self-consciousness is the self-consciousness of a creature, and carries with it an im-

mediate apprehension of the Creator. I know myself as limited and created, dependent upon that which is external to myself and to all other finite beings. The more profoundly I know myself the more vividly I become aware that other things and beings exist and that their power over me is on balance greater than mine over them; further that they like me are limited and finite, so that we are all equally in the hands of the Unlimited and Infinite. "How many ages have passed before the human race was instituted I confess I do not know; but of this I have no doubt, that there exists nothing in the created universe which is co-eternal with the Creator." Thus self-consciousness is also God-consciousness. "In order to know God do not go outside yourself, return to yourself. The dwelling-place of truth is in the inner man. And if you discover your own nature as subject to change, then go beyond that nature. . . . Press on, therefore, towards the source from which the light of reason itself is kindled." [2]

This is the immediate, experiential awareness of the truth of the Christian doctrine of creation, that man is finite, that he is a creature, sustained in every moment by the Creator. It is not a proof, but a *lived awareness*. Schleiermacher, in more poetic terms, points perceptively in the modern period to this same human experience of the religious dimension of existence.

Religion consists in man's becoming conscious of his own limitations, of the fortuitous nature of his life as

[2] *The Christian in Philosophy* (New York: Charles Scribner's Sons, 1951, pp. 44-45.

his being runs its course and silently disappears in the Infinite. It is his giving up all audacious pride, and regarding all individual things, himself included, as being necessarily what they are. It is to live in the endless nature of the Whole, to perceive and divine with quiet reverence the place assigned therein to each and all. It is to have sense and taste for the Infinite, to lie on the bosom of the Universe and feel its boundless life and creative power pulsing within our own. It is to drink in the beauty of the world and be drenched through and through with its spirit. It is devoutly to overhear the All in its expressions and acts, to let oneself be swept away by its influence as we contemplate the wonder of its workings, to discover and love the Spirit pervading the cosmic whole.[3]

At the heart of such an awareness is the intuition of creatureliness, of absolute dependence, of God-consciousness. Yet, despite the fact that this awareness is universally available, what would lead one to the painful and difficult task of so plumbing the self-consciousness for God? Calvin says that man will not, for he wants no part of God.

The Shattering of Self-Sufficiency

It is here that the enigma of creation enters with powerful effect. It is when a threat such as death encounters man with the ruthless promise that this too

[3] Anthological summary in H. R. Mackintosh, *Types of Modern Theology* (London: Nisbet & Co., 1937), pp. 45-46.

shall pass, that nothing to which one has put the blood
and sweat of his endeavor will escape the ravishes of
time—only when this awareness dawns in true force,
will the seeming pleasures of bourgeois existence va-
porize, leaving only the nightmarish awareness that
what we took to be life is a child's game of make-be-
lieve. It is only when we, like "K" in Kafka's *The
Trial*, Rieux in Camus' *The Plague*, Orestes in Sartre's
The Flies, Dmitri in Dostoevsky's *The Brothers Karamazov*, Celia in Eliot's *The Cocktail Party*, have
encountered in despair the vision of life as it is in all
its threatened meaninglessness that we are shaken from
the self-assured posture of the self-willed man that
Calvin knew so well. In being so reduced to size, we
are placed in a situation to see ourselves as we truly
are, to understand from within what it means to exist.
The threat of death can open one to an awareness of
his utter contingency not simply at the end of life, but
in every moment of that life. This is the feeling of
creatureliness. Herein is the illumination that every
moment of life is sheer gift over which one has no control, that one is constantly and absolutely dependent
on a power that is not his own, that he is undergirded
in his freedom by a vitality that is not the self. Such
threat can exhibit man for what he is—*a finite creature*.

It is true, crisis can stimulate escapism, a frantic craving for self-deception. But we are speaking here not of
escaping specific finite threats. We are speaking of the

absolute threat to which such finite threats can open one. Before the abyss which opens to engulf the once "self-sufficient" creature, one finds that he nevertheless continues to exist, despite the fact that he himself has no power, no necessity, no right for existence. Such an apprehension of contingency, of the living self-contradiction contained in the very idea of self-sufficient creatureliness, brings the answer which Tillich calls the awareness of the "power of being." It is to encounter the real mystery of existence, the mystery rooted in the fact that anything exists at all. Existence itself is a mystery. It is this very fact of anything coming into being and remaining in being that can drive a man beyond himself to see the mystery of existence as the finite side of the Divine activity of creation.

Levels of Religious Awareness

Such an encounter with the unique religious depth-dimension of life can differ radically in its degree of intensity. At the minimal level is the intuition of contingency brought about by experiences of finite dependence, evoking the awareness of the absolute contingency of one's own existence. From this awareness of creatureliness one infers the existence of a Creator, for finitude requires the Infinite as its other pole, creature requires Creator.

At the second level of intensity, that testified to by

Schleiermacher, is the experience of the Power of Being as the reverse side of the intuition of contingency. The very life, the very consciousness which is the self, is experienced as radiating with a power not one's own. One now knows from within that he exists only because God is. Human life, by its very fact, testifies to the continuous creative activity of God. This is not, as on the first level, the awareness that God is necessary to account for the intuition of contingency; rather, the intuition of being a creature brings with it the immediate awareness of the co-existence of creature and Creator.

At the third level, pointed to best by such contemporary thinkers as Abraham Heschel and Martin Buber, is the apprehension of the majesty, awe, glory of God as his presence is radiated throughout all creation, from a sublime sunset to the leafy grandeur of a tree. Yet, even this more inclusive awareness has its foundation in the puncturing of man's pride and false autonomy by the intuition of radical contingency. Until man experiences himself from within for what he truly is, one's perception of nature remains only the surface examination proper to the scientific domain.

The fourth level, a level to be accepted (if at all) by the testimony of the few, is that to which the mystics and saints through the centuries have born witness. This level includes both the consuming mystical experience of the *mysterium tremendum,* as Rudolf Otto

GOD AS UNIVERSALLY KNOWABLE

calls it, and the full-blown "religious experience" characteristic of the saint.

With the possible exception of the last level of religious awareness, this experience of the religious dimension of reality is not revelation. It is not a *special* act of Divine Self-Disclosure. It is a religious awareness that is universally available to every man, for it is the dimension or relation in which all stand by the mere fact of their existence. It is not a special revealing activity of God in the world, but the lived-awareness of God's continuous and immediate activity in sustaining the world. Because God is the undergirding power of life, he is immediately present in every life, to be apprehended as the center of every existent thing. It is the relation to God in which one *already* stands, whether one knows it or not. God is forever there, nearer than self, to be apprehended.

The fact that not all men perceive this truth in no way disproves the universality of this religious dimension of creation. All who have known great music realize that everyone has the potentiality for entering into an aesthetic experience with, for example, Bach's *Brandenburg Concerti* or Beethoven's *Kreutzer Sonata*. But does everyone so enter? Clearly not. In music, many of us have not gotten past the level of John Philip Sousa. Yet this in no way means that such individuals are incapable of profound aesthetic experience. It means, rather, that they have never really been opened to such a relation. With preparation, with increased exposure, one can be brought from Belafonte through Tschaikovsky's *1812 Overture* to the fullness of aesthetic perception.

Likewise in the religious dimension, the relation is there to be apprehended, for man by the fact of his existence already stands in the creation-relation of creature to Creator. Unlike other relations, however, the religious awareness effects a total reorientation of the self, for it thrusts upon man the role of creature, a role that punctures all false superiority and self-idolatry. It is inevitable that this is an awareness that man tends to fight unto death. Yet before the specter of death, one must abandon all pretense and bow to his true nature in creation. To realize that death is the one fact to which man cannot say NO is to understand that what is true at the moment of death is true of every moment of life. We neither create nor sustain our life. I exist only because there is a mysterious depth that is the Ground of my being. It is this awareness that the enigma of creation is opening in our time, short of the moment of death itself.

*   *   *

Our task in this chapter began with the question, "Does the nature of the world give us any certain knowledge that it is created, that the existence of God can be proved?" Upon exploring the proofs, three points emerged.

First, in speaking of a "First Cause," the proofs could not mean that the scientific question of "how" logically requires an ancient mover to complete the historical account of the emergence of the world. The religious First Cause is an answer to a quite different question.

Second, in speaking of God, the question is not whether one should believe in a God or no God. The question is whether the "god" in relation to which one necessarily finds his meaning for living is the highest that existence can support. Since the "god" of human life, however, tends to be one's own self, belief in the God of theism is not really a question of evidence but a question regarding man's will. The proofs, even if logically correct, are powerless to reorient a "self-sufficient" individual.

The third point of importance concerned the distinction drawn by many philosophers and scientists between phenomenon and noumenon, between things as they appear to be, and things as they are in themselves, unaltered by the human perspective. Although we may agree concerning the ways in which various things appear, one cannot move logically from this knowledge to any certainty about the ultimate nature and meaning of all things.

With the problem of the knowledge of God at this seeming agnostic impasse, our attempt was to show that what such thinking was actually pointing to was the existence of various legitimate experiences of various dimensions of reality. One of these is the religious, pointed to by the ultimate question, WHY?, or again, "What does it mean to exist?"

The skepticism that haunts modern man in his search for ultimate meaning has its source in the fact that the knower and the known are separated, strangers, unlikes. But in one case, the case of the self delving into its own depths, subject and object are identical. One cannot prove the conclusions of such introspection; it is more a matter of capturing the "feel" of existence, what it is like to be a man. This one can know only for himself, by drinking deeply and self-consciously of life.

Yet man is cursed by a complacency, by a self-satisfaction that demands neither depth nor seriousness. The mass man is a man characterized by conformity, by unquestioning acceptance, lulled by the sweet forgetfulness of habit. The serious and agonizing birth of self-consciousness in depth that is the origin of religious awareness is not freely chosen. The religious quest is begun only if one can do no other, only if there is a need that haunts and permits no rest.

As a result, although the demonic aspects of creation dawning upon our generation are a haunting problem for traditional religion, this same fact can drive modern man to the awareness of his contingency, his ultimate dependence for every moment of existence on a power not his own.

This is not revelation, but a human awareness, an understanding from within of the God-dependence in which one now stands, whether he acknowledges it or not.

It is at this point that the question of revelation arises, for the searcher for ultimate meaning must ask: is this religious awareness sufficient?

4
CREATION
AND THE SEARCH
FOR BIBLICAL MEANING

> We are the dispossessed—the dispossessed of faith;
> the physically or spiritually homeless. . . . Let me be-
> lieve in something.
> —Arthur Koestler, *The Age of Longing* [1]

THROUGH THE ENIGMA OF CREATION, man can be
brought to an awareness of the religious dimension, the
relation of creatureliness in which all finite reality
stands for its existence. Yet when one is dealing with
the realm of religious intuition or experience within
the depths of the self, one is not dealing with the clear,
the easily analyzed and understood. It is an apprehension rather than a comprehension; it is a preconceptual
awareness.

The next step in our explorations is to understand
how this religious intuition comes to greater clarity
and perhaps fuller certainty when further confirmed
by the co-operating witness to God gathered from the

[1] New York: The Macmillan Company, 1959.

external world. In fact, the intuition of contingency might die and never come to conscious realization unless strengthened by such external evidence.

VALUE OF THE PROOFS

In the Middle Ages, the kind of knowledge sought was absolute, certain knowledge. Many regarded such knowledge as provided for theism by the traditional proofs. This was an error that in time became most clear.

Much of the criticism of religion in the early days of science rested in the fact that when contrasted with the "certain" knowledge gained through the scientific method, the traditional proofs were anemic indeed. In our own times, however, scientists have seen clearly that even the laws of nature are not certain but forever probable. Since this is the case with even scientific knowledge, it is hardly to be required that human knowledge in the realm of religion must be radically different. All human knowledge is a matter of conclusions drawn in terms of converging probabilities.

This everyday method for deriving truth finds its most distinguished example in the judicial system. The task of a jury is to determine guilt "without a reasonable doubt." The manner in which such a conclusion is reached is in terms of converging or cumulative probability. The proximity of the suspect to the mur-

der scene is not sufficient for conviction. Neither is the
fact that he owns a gun of the same caliber as the murder weapon, or that blood was discovered on one of his
shirts. Other such facts could be discovered, none of
which in themselves prove anything. And yet, when
taken together not as a logical argument but in terms
of the impact which they cumulatively produce, the
jury "without a reasonable doubt" demands the life of
the accused.

In like manner, the traditional arguments fail as rational proofs (the arguments from movement, from
causality, from evidence of design seen in the world,
the experiences of beauty and morality). Yet when
these are regarded in terms of cumulative probability,
just as knowledge in other realms is gained, they become quite persuasive in supporting the experience of
contingency.

The contemporary philosopher, J. J. C. Smart, has
spoken perceptively of one of these arguments:

> The argument from design is no good as an argument.
> But in those who have the seeds of a genuinely religious
> attitude already within them the facts to which the
> argument from design draws attention, facts showing
> the grandeur and majesty of the universe, facts that are
> evident to anyone who looks upwards on a starry night,
> and which are enormously multiplied for us by the ad-
> vance of theoretical science, these facts have a power-
> ful effect. But they only have this effect on the already
> religious mind, on the mind which has the capability

of feeling the religious type of awe. That is, the argument from design is in reality no argument, or if it is regarded as an argument it is feeble, but it is a potent instrument in heightening religious emotions.[2]

It has been our insistence that this religious awareness is open to everyone who is made aware of the human situation. Consequently, the approach from design, as from the other cosmological approaches, can be a very powerful vehicle not only in opening the religious inquirer to the probability of God's existence, but in evoking the intuitive awareness of the Creator. In fact, the religious intuition is probably never divorced from one's feeling for the possibility or probability of God on the basis of external evidence; likewise, external evidence is probably never entertained seriously unless one is threatened by meaninglessness in his own personal life. And, in the end, this threat of meaninglessness is probably never present without some feeling, however dim, for one's own contingency before a power not one's own. In the religious search, these elements work together in a kind of dialogue.

THE NATURE OF THE CREATOR

The religious quest for ultimate meaning does not end here. In fact, this is only its beginning. Although

[2] A. Flew & A. MacIntyre (eds.), *New Essays in Philosophical Theology* (London: SCM Press, 1955), p. 45. Permission granted by The Macmillan Company, New York.

the existence of God can be experientially certain, it is the *nature* of this God that quickly becomes the key issue if one is to discover the purpose, the meaning, of the divinely creative venture of existence in which one is participating.

It is this method of cumulative probability that is of crucial importance in bringing a partial answer to this question. Without religious intuition, the approach to theism can be only in terms of probability. Once the intuition of contingency dawns, however, the case from cumulative probability is reversed. One's concern is no longer with the probability of God's *existence* but with probability concerning his *nature*. If God exists, if he is the Ground which sustains all things in existence, then the world and its ingredients become an indication of what the Creator God is like. As the philosopher J. E. Smith says,

> No complete idea of God is possible apart from considering the structure of the world and even of cultural-historical existence. . . . The nature of God is given throughout the full range of finite being, and such being must be consulted at every level if we are to be clear about the meaning of the divine attributes.[3]

One cannot know the goal that gives meaning to the whole of creation simply by experiencing one's self as dependent in each moment upon God. Only by con-

[3] "The Present Status of Natural Theology," *Journal of Philosophy*, LV, No. 22 (Oct., 1958), 935.

sulting the historical and cosmic processes from the perspective of the certainty that God exists can we perceive the novel in the linear sweep that indicates purpose. Just as the intuition of God emerges through a dialogue with external reality, so the search for the nature of God is a dialogue between the intuition of contingency and the external world.

In moving toward the existence of God, the case from cumulative probability consults the external world, noting evidence for the probability of a moral God in the experience of moral demands, a God of purpose and intelligence in the design and direction of the cosmic process, a God who is the fullness of Being in the values, beauty, and orderliness of the world. Once one comes to the immediate certainty of the existence of such a Divine Ground, this evidence becomes a basis for understanding the Divine Nature. Once one believes in God, one's perspective toward all reality is radically changed. Now one looks at the world as the plane of God's activity in which there is nothing positive in being which is not ultimately according to his will. This new perspective is not only intellectual, but it involves the whole man. One's moral, aesthetic, and cognitive sensitivities are shaken from the charge of being only subjective. They become instruments to plumb the depths of existence for understanding ultimate meaning, that is, for understanding the nature of God. This immediacy with the richness of life can grow so as to transform increasingly the individual as it transforms his view of all reality.

THE INSUFFICIENCY OF THE RELIGIOUS AWARENESS

Yet the matter cannot rest here. The Christian, through the years, has insisted that God is not unitarian, but Trinitarian. This insistence is far from an irrelevant dissection of God. It rests on the awareness that the intuitive experience of God is not sufficient in itself. The intuitive awareness of contingency is based upon the awareness of God as Creator. This is what every man is capable of intuiting, because he is dependent on this relationship of creation for his very existence.

The Christian insists, however, that God is also Redeemer and Inspirer. This is what is meant in talking of God as God the Father, God the Son, and God the Holy Spirit—God revealing himself in three distinct modes of activity. The Trinity is not a blueprint of the Divine Psyche, but a confession about the richness of God's relation to man, a richness based on man's experience of Him. To understand what it could mean to confess God as Redeemer and Inspirer, we must uncover what it is that forces a man beyond the intuitive awareness of the Creator to other modes of Divine activity as necessary for a final solution to the religious question.

The Problem of Evil

The first problem driving man to a consideration of Christian revelation is the problem of evil. The conclusion to be drawn from the intuitive awareness of God would seem to be that God is the Creator of all, that in coming to creative fullness all things satisfy the Will and intent of the Creator. Can one escape the conclusion, then, that while man expresses the Will of God in his finite act of being a man, so also does the microbe in being a microbe and killing the man express the Will of the Creator? From the perspective of our religious answer thus far, it is difficult to conclude otherwise than that God is no more than equally concerned on both sides. One can, of course, draw probable arguments in favor of providence or grace, thereby tipping the scale, but it is always possible to offer counterarguments that are highly disturbing.

Likewise, there is always the problem of death. Does the fact that God is the Ground of all things in existence give any guarantee that death is not final? Austin Farrer's conclusion to his own rational case for theism puts the matter well:

As I wrote this, the German armies were occupying Paris, after a campaign prodigal of blood and human distress. Rational theology will not tell us whether this has or has not been an unqualified and irretrievable disaster to mankind and especially to the men who died. It is another matter, if we believe that God Incarnate also died and rose from the dead. But rational theology knows only that whether Paris stands or falls, whether men die or live, God is God, and so long as any spiritual creature survives, God is to be adored.[4]

If God is equally concerned with all beings and with all events, the problem of evil becomes severe, and, from this human perspective, omnipresent Divine Creativity can quickly take on the hallmarks of cosmic indifference.

From man's finite perspective, the problem of evil will never be completely solved either from the position of theism or from the atheistic conclusion. The real problem is, How can one live creatively in its presence? Nietzsche put his finger at the heart of the problem when he said, "It isn't the suffering itself which I find unbearable, but the meaninglessness of it all." Consequently, if God is active on man's behalf, if God himself is engaged in the cosmic battle with evil, if he is capable and willing to bring good from evil, then the problem of evil is put on a totally different plane.

This is what the Christian insists as being true as he points at the Incarnation; it is a point made most powerfully in the report of Father Panteloux's sermon in Camus' *The Plague:*

[4] *Finite and Infinite* (London: A. & C. Black Ltd., Dacre Press; and Naperville, Ill.: Alec R. Allenson, Inc., 1959), p. 300.

Nothing was more important on earth than a child's suffering, the horror it inspires in us, and the reasons we must find to account for it. In other manifestations of life God made things easy for us and, thus far, our religion had no merit. But in this respect He put us, so to speak, with our backs to the wall. Indeed, we all were up against the wall that plague had built around us, and in its lethal shadow we must work out our salvation. He, Father Paneloux, refused to have recourse to simple devices enabling him to scale that wall. Thus he might easily have assured them that the child's sufferings would be compensated for by an eternity of bliss awaiting him. But how could he give that assurance when, to tell the truth, he knew nothing about it? For who would dare to assert that eternal happiness can compensate for a single moment's human suffering? He who asserted that would not be a true Christian, a follower of the Master who knew all the pangs of suffering in his body and his soul. No, he, Father Paneloux, would keep faith with that great symbol of all suffering, the tortured body on the Cross; he would stand fast, his back to the wall, and face honestly the terrible problem of a child's agony.[5]

It is in the cross that the Christian sees the most profound portrait of God. What is revealed is not simply God the Creator, the Ground of Being. In this Incarnate Figure he sees God the sufferer, the God who has willed to undergo all the horrors of finite evil, the God who is forever active toward man with infinite

[5] *The Plague* (New York: Alfred A. Knopf, Inc., 1957), pp. 201-202.

compassion and ultimate concern. Here is God the "Unmoved Mover" revealed as the most "moved" of Movers. In seeing here the most powerful portrait of *Divine* Love, the man of faith can believe that love undergirds suffering and evil. Through the Resurrection comes the certainty that love has the last word, that death is overcome and infinite good is brought out of evil. This is not all that can be said concerning evil, nor all that we shall say, but through such revelation the problem of evil is transposed into a new key. In Christ, solution by theory, hypothesis, and probability is transcended by Divine *Fact*, and a human problem becomes also a Divine Problem, for God himself is active within it.

At this point we are not attempting to defend the truth of the Christian revelation, but only to show that such revelation, *if* true, is a significant addition to the understanding of the Creator gained through the awareness of contingency.

The Problem of Human "Sin"

The second reason for insisting upon the need for God as Redeemer involves the problem of "sin." Looked at in one way, the intuition of contingency is an awareness of infinite meaning, for it is the awareness that creative purpose undergirds life. And yet, regarded in another way, such knowledge comes as damning judgment. Paul made this clear in speaking of revelation—before God's law was revealed to me, he lamented, I was without sin. If God does not exist, ultimately there is no such thing as good and evil, except in the easy sense of arbitrary civil law. But once the demanding Will of God is known, man stands condemned.

This is analogous to the awareness of God as Creator. Through religious intuition one comes to the awareness that in becoming a man, in fulfilling one's potentialities, in expressing his nature in its fullness, he is doing the Will of the Creator God. One is continuing the Divine Creativity. From the perspective of this awareness, however, one is forced to recognize that his life to this very point has been one of seeking elemental satisfactions at the expense of his higher nature. He stands guilty of living a lie, of denying in act and in consciousness the existence of Him without whom he would not even be. Despite certain contemporary theologians, the fact that God continues to sustain man even in his unbelief is in no way a basis for believing that one stands forgiven and accepted by God, that his rebellion against the Creator is not counted against him.

What is needed in such a situation is a *new* relation between God and man. We see this to be true in the finite realm. In perpetrating a genuine injustice against another person, there is no way for this relation to become vital and meaningful again unless the injured is willing to extend forgiveness and acceptance. It is here that we get to the heart of the Protestant insistence that God's revelation in Jesus Christ provides the only "saving" knowledge. Unless God moves specially toward me, forgives me *in particular*, then the God-man relation of creation, even if recognized, is a relation of estrangement, of judgment, in which I stand guilty of forfeiting the meaning which comes from the existence of God.

This is what Augustine meant when he said that all that the Christian affirms could be discovered without need of special revelation, all things but one—"The Word made flesh." Only in the Incarnation, consummated in the Crucifixion and Resurrection, is the *new* relation of forgiveness brought into being. Such forgiveness becomes valid only when the inspiration of God the Holy Spirit brings one to the immediate awareness that God's act in Jesus Christ not simply occurred, but occurred for me. An invitation must be personally extended before it has anything to do with me.

It is for this reason that Christians have insisted upon God as Redeemer and as Holy Spirit if the awareness of God as Creator is to be more than judgment. Although it is necessary that God exists because man exists, there is no necessity involved in God's forgiveness. To forgive is to say, "Nevertheless." It is a disregard of logic in a free act of love. Consequently, since forgiveness is not necessary, not logically required, human reason can neither know God's forgiveness nor in any way lay claim upon it. It is a Willed Act by God, and it is in this quality of being a free act that Divine Forgiveness becomes miraculous.

The Problem of Human Impotence

The second basic reason for insisting upon the need for God's triune activity is closely related to a third—the problem of human "impotence." A realistic appraisal of man indicates that the center of man's being is not reason but will. As Calvin insisted, man denies God not because it is rational to do so, but because man wills himself to be supreme. As a result, one's reason becomes intent not on discovering the truth but on rationalizing this assertion of will.

The use of reason today to justify the selfish ends of diverse agencies, from the demands of labor to the sales techniques of management, gives ample testimony to man's subtle ability to pervert reason by making it an unconscious tool for irrational self-aggrandizement. Even though the enigma of creation may be powerful enough to shake man from this self-elevation, at least sufficiently for the recognition of one's creatureliness, the words of Paul are haunting: "I can will what is right, but I cannot do it. For I do not do the good I

want, but the evil I do not want is what I do. . . .
Wretched man that I am! Who will deliver me from
this body of death?" (Romans 7:18-19, 24). Even *if*
one comes to recognize the existence of God, and sees
clearly what this existence requires, and even *if* he
comes to will with his mind to do this, he finds that he
is a divided creature. One's being is so set on itself that
he cannot help making himself first even in the attempt
to act selflessly. William Temple, in *Nature, Man and
God*, puts the problem well:

> *Self-determination is the characteristic of man as a
> moral being, and without it he could never be called
> into fellowship with God. But it is not the last word of
> human development; on the contrary it contains the
> sentence of endless frustration as truly as it affords the
> opportunity of entry upon the spiritual enterprise. For
> the self which determines cannot carry the self which is
> determined above its own level.*[6]

Loss of self-centeredness, of self-deification, is possible only through a special act of God. It is utterly
impossible for the selfish will to selfishly will to be
selfless. Such a Divine Act must not destroy human
freedom, but must be so dramatic that it can evoke a
response which elevates man out of himself. He must
be freed from himself in order to become free—that is,
free to fulfill his essence, his nature, to become the
Divinely oriented creature he was created to become.

[6] New York: The Macmillan Company, 1953.

Revelation as Verification

The final reason for special revelation involves the matter of verification. If God exists, and he is no less than the creation which he undergirds, we are led forcefully to expect a personal revelation of himself and his cosmic purpose. Without special revelation, God's silence appears as a contradiction to his existence; with revelation, the case for theism is completed as one has been led all the way along the line to expect.

CHRISTIAN REVELATION AND THE WORLD'S RELIGIONS

When the religious searcher is forced to consider seriously the question of special revelation, however, he encounters, disconcertingly, a panorama of various religions, each claiming for itself some special knowledge or indispensable mandate from the Divine which alone is true. Spokesmen for the Judeo-Christian tradition have likewise, at times, made exclusive claims, often to the point of undermining the love which is at the heart of its proclamations.

At the very beginning of Christianity, however, precedent was set in regard to other religions that was far more commensurate with its message. Jesus said, "I have other sheep, that are not of this fold; I must bring them also, and they will heed my voice. So there shall be one flock, one shepherd." (John 10:16) In this spirit, Paul mounted Mars Hill and addressed the Greeks:

> Men of Athens, I perceive that in every way you are very religious. For as I passed along, and observed the objects of your worship, I found also an altar with this inscription, "To an unknown God." What therefore you worship as unknown, this I proclaim unto you." (Acts 17:22-23)

In most cases, Christianity has become sterile, often self-contradictory, when it has attempted to transform a confession of faith into a logical doctrine. So is the case here. In the Judeo-Christian tradition, consummated in Jesus Christ, the Christian finds a full and total revelation of God himself, of his purposes and activity with men. This in no way entails a condemnation of other faiths. God is universally knowable, and he has not left himself without witnesses in any place. What the Christian confesses is that all that man needs, God has done in Jesus Christ, that no more complete revelation is possible after the Incarnation. What the Christian is called to do is to share this love he has known by bringing others to a wholeness they have never known, by bringing partial religious awarenesses to completion, or simply by sharing that which cannot be held but possessed only in being given away.

In the end, the Christian in regard to other religions can only confess in love, "As for me and my house, Jesus Christ is the final and complete revelation of

God; enter and find the God of love, that none may go away unsatisfied." More than this is the rivalry of sects, a glorification of man rather than God, a love of self rather than neighbor.

Therefore, the Christian can in no way prove that the revelation in which he believes is the only revelation. What he must do is to so present the meaning of the biblical revelation that the searcher may see it as the completion of his quest. To this task we now turn.

The "Truth-Relation" and the "Meaning-Relation"

There is no proving the truth of Christian revelation. Indeed, since its truth is a relation that is new, it is true only for one for whom God makes it true. To know of a dance is not to be invited. Unfortunately, however, many Christians understand this to mean that Scripture, the record of God's revelation through his "mighty acts in history," is closed to all except the believer. If this were the case, our search for ultimate meaning would come to a frustrating end. Any conclusion to our quest, if it has one, would be exclusively God's doing and his alone.

What we must show now is that the Scripture is available to the unbeliever as an indispensable instrument in his search. The task of the Christian is not to prove the truth of Christian revelation but to exhibit

its meaning. This distinction between "truth" and
"meaning" in one's relation to Scripture is of fundamental importance in approaching Christianity.

It is obvious that personal commitment to the truth
of Scripture is necessary for one to affirm the biblical
meaning as true for one's self. But what must be seen is
that even without commitment to its truth, one can
participate in the meaning of the biblical world-view.
The fundamental issue involved here is whether it is
possible for one to operate from the perspective of a
world-view without necessarily accepting this perspective as true for one's self. Can one, regardless of
his present ultimate commitment, by an act of conscious intent, participate for at least a short time in the
"religious mind-set," the "historical perspective," the
"existential theological involvement," call it what you
will, of the writers of the biblical material? Unless this
is possible, Scripture is closed to the nonbeliever; it
cannot be a vehicle in coming to faith, and revelation
undercuts human freedom by making of no consequence the human search for biblical faith.

It is through one's capacities for aesthetic relations
that such a participation in meaning is possible. The
definition provided by Eliseo Vivas in his *Creation and
Discovery* is to the point: "An aesthetic experience is
an experience of rapt attention which involves the
intransitive apprehension of an object's immanent
meanings and values in their full presentational imme-

diacy." [7] What is meant is that in great poetry, for example, the reader participates in and becomes a part of the poem's "world." As long as this relationship is aesthetic, the question of truth or falsity is irrelevant, for it is suspended. Vivas calls aesthetic experience the "suspension of disbelief," for through it one becomes absorbed in the world-view of the artist's creation.

The implications of this human capacity for our problem are not hard to see. The Christian insists that there is a human nature common to all men. This universal nature provides a common basis for human involvement with the perennial questions of existence which transcend time, tradition, and place. Even the atheist Sartre, while denying such a common human essence, provides a universal basis for aesthetic participation by insisting upon a human situation common to ancient Hebrew, first century Galilean, and modern man alike. It is for either reason or both that in a great drama, the life portrayed becomes for the duration of the aesthetic act *my* life. In a real sense, I am Hamlet and Hamlet is I. Although I may personally disagree vehemently with every aspect of Sartre's philosophy, through such a dramatic work as *The Flies*, I know from within what it means to be an atheistic existentialist.

T. S. Eliot once said that it is through theology that

[7] New York: Noonday Press, Inc., 1955.

what the Christian believes to be true can be known,
but it is through Christian drama that what it means to
be a Christian can be experienced. In like manner, the
search for ultimate meaning requires that the meaning
of the biblical world-view, the "drama of God's mighty
acts in history," be experienced, not necessarily as
one's own, but experienced with such a dramatic immediacy that one participates in that meaning from
within.

This crucial distinction between "aesthetic" and
"existential" involvement receives significant confir-
mation from the great Protestant thinker, Søren
Kierkegaard (1813-1855). Kierkegaard severely at-
tacked the aesthetic view of life, from the perspective
of the religious. Through the aesthetic, he stated, it is
possible for one to participate in religious realities
without ever being committed to their truth. This is
precisely what we are affirming; but viewing this human capacity, not as a way of life but as a way of discovering meaning, it must be seen in the most positive
way.

It is in this manner that the Scripture can be opened
to the unbeliever so that it may speak for itself. The
unbeliever can make the transition from understanding
the meaning of revelation to affirming its truth only if
he is led through the aesthetic encounter to the awareness that the spirit in which he is participating is in
truth the Spirit by which one is called. From the side

of the searcher for meaning, one is grasped aesthetically by the New Testament portrait of Jesus as the Christ; from the side of the believer, the searcher is grasped by God-in-Christ and Christ-in-God. This transition from meaning to truth is often quite gradual, but the difference which the transition makes in the life of the individual is such that the believer must confess: "I could not have chosen Thee, had Thou not first chosen me." The most that the Christian can do as an instrument in God's seeking is to offer the Scriptures to the unbeliever for this aesthetic participation, hacking down the intruding barriers which the individual brings to block such a relation. Only God the Holy Spirit can bring one from meaning to truth.

It is because of this human capacity for aesthetic involvement that one of the most perceptive interpreters of Christianity in our day is the nonbeliever, Albert Camus. Camus does not reject Christianity as meaningless, irrelevant, and worthless to modern man. Rather, it is Camus' insistence that the world-view of Christianity is the most meaningful affirmation imaginable, one which would provide the answer to the enigma of creation for which he so desperately searched—it would, that is, *if true.* Camus was never able himself to make the transition from meaning to truth, but the meaning, the relevance, of Christianity to the problems of man, he never doubted.

THE UNITY OF THE BIBLE

Let us now see what is involved in an aesthetic participation in Scripture. As the reader, aware of the human dilemma in which he stands and the questions that permit no rest, attempts in his search for answer to enter into a meaning-relation with Scripture, the immediate problem is the specter of sixty-six separate books, written over a long span of time by a plurality of authors on a plurality of themes. How is it possible for one to enter into the world-view of the Bible?

There is emerging in our day a discipline called "biblical theology," based on the insight that, despite this plurality, there is a basic unity to the Bible. "Unity," here, can mean two things. First, it can be understood as meaning a significant similarity between the theologies and specific "doctrines" of the various biblical writers. In this sense, it is clear that there is no biblical theology, only biblical theologies, for there is a significant development and perhaps even conflict in theological understanding among the various writers. But unity may also mean a "faith-orientation" which so permeates the thought of each biblical writer that the individual theologies can be seen as direct products of the individual writers, grounded in this abiding faith-perspective, encountering their own peculiar situations with the question, "What does this faith mean for our age?" This is a unity of tradition, but tradition understood not in terms of common dogmatic formulations. It is tradition understood as an orienting "frame of reference" arising from the personal participation of each writer in the religious community of Israel in which this tradition lived and was strangely present.

This biblical faith-perspective cannot be fully expressed in words, for it is a living relation in which one must participate, at least aesthetically, in order to understand. Yet this faith-perspective (world-view) can be pointed to evocatively by means of *grund motifs*, recurring themes, which, while they are not this grounding faith, are symbols pointing to it. Although these motifs evolved significantly throughout biblical history, they are so imbedded in this unifying faith-basis that they provide a wholeness underlying particular theological expressions in various biblical epochs.

Although there are a number of such motifs that can be uncovered in Scripture, there are two in particular which are basic for communicating the meaning of the faith-perspective from which the Jew and Christian wrote and understood their Scriptures. The motif most fundamental to the Old Testament and the Jewish world-view is the motif, "Creation for Covenant." This motif was incorporated vitally into the overarching motif characterizing the New Testament and the Christian world-view, "Creation for Incarnation."

It is within these fundamental rubrics that the fuller meaning of creation for the Christian must be understood. It is through aesthetic participation in the faith-perspective to which these motifs point that the biblical meaning encounters the searcher for truth in his crisis-involvement with the human dilemma.

*   *   *

Our search for ultimate meaning has indicated the availability of a human awareness of contingency through which the existence of the Creator can be affirmed. And yet this affirmation has not proved sufficient.

Although the traditional "proofs" can be of supplementary help in providing cumulative probability concerning God's existence and nature, there are some haunting questions that still remain. The God who creates and the evil in creation—how can the head-on conflict between these two realities possibly be resolved? Further, to come to acknowledge the Creator God is to come to recognize one's own sin, one's own rebellion and betrayal of Him without whom one would not even be. "If Thou, O Lord, shouldst mark iniquities, Lord, who could stand?" (Psalms 130:3).

Yet even to realize one's rebellion is not sufficient, for it is the agony of human life that the self is divided against itself. One need not move beyond New Year's resolutions to realize the chasm that divides performance from good intention.

It is such questions as these that drive the searcher

for ultimate meaning to consider seriously the answers which Christians claim come from biblical revelation. One must see immediately, however, that truth in the religious sense does not mean simply assenting to dogmas or creedal statements, as one would assent to the statement that Australia is an island, even though he has never sailed around it. Religious truth means that to which my total self is oriented, that which I trust unto death, that from which I draw the meaning that shapes my life and its activities.

Obviously, one cannot give truth in this sense to another person through logic or proof. To affirm something, not as being true in general, but as being true for me, I must enter into a living relation with it, and feel its claim laid upon me.

Many Christians understand this to mean that Christian faith is either given to a man or it is withheld, and all human effort toward it is vain. Man's capacity for entering into aesthetic relations, however, is such that this conclusion does not seem called for. In an aesthetic relation one can participate in the meaning of something without being committed to its truth. It is this ability that makes it possible for the searcher to enter into the meaning of the biblical world-view, to see existence from within the faith-orientation of revelation. One can gain a "feel" for the meaning with which Christian revelation can imbue one's life. He can know from within what it means to be a Christian.

More than this a man cannot do, for the transition between the statement, "I know what it means," and the confession, "In this truth I believe," is the mystery that marks the work of the Holy Spirit. B. W. Anderson's comments in *Rediscovering the Bible* are to the point:

> If we are to hear God's Word spoken through the Bible to our situation today, our first task is to put ourselves within the world of the Bible. . . . We must live with the Bible until it becomes part of us, just as the actor identifies himself with the role that he plays. It is then, perhaps, that the Holy Spirit, breathing through the ancient words of the sacred page, will lead us to know that the "Word of the Lord" spoken by the prophets and embodied in Jesus Christ is actually the deepest interpretation of our own life situation and our world crisis in the twentieth century.[8]

In entering into a "meaning-relation" with the biblical world-view, there is no substitute for direct encounter with the biblical writings themselves. And yet one is greatly aided in this participation by having pointed out to him the orienting motif(s) that unify these writings as an expression of a total way of life. For the Jew, such a motif is "Creation for Covenant." For the Christian, such a faith-orientation is fulfilled in the more inclusive motif, "Creation for Incarnation."

It is to an understanding of this meaning that we

[8] (New York: Association Press, 1951), p. 22.

now turn in the following chapters, attempting above all to remove the needless stumbling blocks that have made the Christian world-view seem so impossible for many modern men.

CREATION

5 FOR COVENANT AND FOR INCARNATION

___

> By God's taking thought for man in Jesus Christ,
> now as in the past, He has provided knowledge
> about the creating, sustaining and governing of the
> world and man, and about His glory and ours.
> —Karl Barth, *The Knowledge of God and the
> Service of God* [1]

IT SHOULD NOW BE CLEAR to the reader that the Hebraic interest in creation was not that of scientific curiosity. Rather, it was a religious concern with ultimate
meaning. The ingredients of the Hebraic world-view
emerged over a long period of time. Consequently,
they ranged in nature from prehistorical legend and
mythology to carefully recorded historical fact. These
ingredients were drawn from experiences unique to the
Jews and from experiences imbedded in the general
folklore of the region.

Although these diverse sources are certainly discernible, there is in Scripture what we can best call an edi-

[1] Naperville, Ill.: Alec R. Allenson, 1955.

torial unity. The "authors" or editors of the various books sought the relevance and meaning of these various sources by understanding them and reworking them from the perspective of the unique historical experiences of the Israelites. Likewise, from this faith-perspective the Jews viewed the present world around them, attempting to discover and live the ultimate meaning thereby exhibited in all things, from their social, political, and economic relations to the menial tasks of every household.

THE PRIMITIVE BIBLICAL SOURCES

In the process of Hebraic history this faith-perspective grew more profound and rich, but not in the sense that the basic underlying faith changed. Rather, this faith-perspective enlarged and became more mature as it further participated in the ongoing relation of Divine Action and human reaction. It was in this way that even those materials which were borrowed in rather wholesale fashion from surrounding traditions were significantly reworked until the original intent of this material was often lost and the total meaning altered.

Examples of this transposition can be seen in the second creation narrative of Genesis (2:4-4:16). In this story of the Garden of Eden we find various explanatory legends, primitive explanations that are indelibly marked as belonging to the early thought of man. In this one account we find "explanations" for man's wearing of apparel, for woman's abnormal fear of snakes, for the lowly estate of women, for the existence of thorns and thistles, for the pain of woman in childbirth, for why the snake crawls on its stomach, along with many more "explanations" that are not so easily recognized. Throughout Genesis we have legends accounting for wells, peculiar geological formations, forgotten towers, and the like.

The Editorial Unity of the Bible

Later in Jewish history, writers came to sense in the ancient words and stories greater meaning and significance than the more primitive mind had detected. By the time that the book of Genesis was finally collected and edited, the primitive material had been molded into a unique whole by those immersed in the self-conscious faith-perspective created by the primary historical events of the Israelite people.

The central events of Hebraic history were God's calling forth of the Jews from Egypt through the person of Moses, their delivery from extermination by the miracle of the Red Sea, the Divine disciplining of Israel through their wanderings in the desert, and finally the establishment of Israel as a nation in the promised land. And why? The faith-answer which Israel made molded all of Jewish history. God's actions were for the purpose of establishing a "covenant" between God and the Hebrews.

THE COVENANT-CALLING

It was the living faith of these people that they had been called for a special destiny; they were the chosen people. Jeremiah states it best: "I will be your God and you shall be my people" (7:23). What this covenant demanded of the Jews in the long run or what the end goal of this covenant might be, were matters not clearly known. What was believed was that God had promised a great destiny to his people. It was faith in this promise of God that gave to these people a meaning that defied all temporal handicaps.

The word "covenant" itself means "artificial brotherhood," to regard another as a brother even though he is not so by nature. A covenant creates both rights and duties, though not necessarily making the two parties equal. The duties which the Covenant placed upon Israel were contained in the law as delivered at Mount Sinai (Exodus 19:4-8). What Israel would "gain" through this obedience was largely left open-ended (Genesis 6:17-22; II Chronicles 15:12). Instead of a clearly defined goal in history, at the heart of the Covenant was an overwhelming sense of Divine Providence, of God's immediate guidance in *all* activities

(Genesis 22:8ff; Nehemiah 9:21). ". . . be not fright-
ened, neither be dismayed; for the Lord your God is
with you wherever you go" (Joshua 1:9). Abraham,
the father of the Covenant, began his response to
God's call to follow in this fashion: ". . . he went out
not knowing where he was to go" (Hebrews 11:8).
The law was not to be an end in itself but was to be a
form of discipline, a preparedness, through which the
Jew was brought to place his *total* reliance upon God's
Will, God's strength, and God's loving companionship
(Deuteronomy 8:1f; Psalms 20:7). It was in this spirit
that the psalmist wrote, "Teach me to do thy will, for
thou art my God" (143:10). The basis for this obedience was an overwhelming gratitude for God's mighty
providential acts in the past (Deuteronomy 15:15).
Thou shalt obey My law, for "I am the Lord your
God, who brought you out of the land of Egypt, out
of the house of bondage" (Exodus 20:2).

BETRAYAL OF THE COVENANT

Whenever tragedy befell, it was understood by the
prophets as the result of Israel's betrayal of the Covenant—man's faithlessness in the face of God's absolute
loyalty, man's reliance upon himself, his own strength,
his own intelligence, his own purposes (Amos 3, Hosea 2, Jeremiah 7). Instead of being an instrument of
God's Will, Israel was found guilty of using God for

man's own ends. We see this, for example, in the warnings of the prophets against Israel's reliance on alliances
with foreign powers, for such covenanting with men
was an open confession of doubt in the providential
power of God (Isaiah 30:1-5; Amos 6:13; Hosea
7:11). We see this in the early prophetic judgments
against Israel's flirtations with the gods of the surrounding peoples. These prophets were not always sure
that other gods did not exist, but to worship them was
wrong, not because they were nonexistent, but because
such worship was a betrayal of the Covenant, a weak-
ening of faith in Israel's God as supreme, a doubting
that God was able to do what he had promised (Judges
8:33).

PERVERSION OF THE COVENANT

In time, many in Israel came to regard the Covenant
as the guarantee that God would do *Israel's* bidding,
rather than a pledge of Israel's total obedience. For
these, the goal of the Covenant was no longer open-
ended, but it was closed and narrowly defined. The
supreme goal of the Covenant was now seen as Israel's
earthly prosperity and sovereignty above every other
nation, to rule and to perpetrate on others that which
others had caused the Hebrews to endure (Amos 5:
18-20). The reoccurring tendency throughout Jewish
history was the attempt to make self and nation first,

even before God himself—the personal and national attempt to *become God* (Jeremiah 7:16-34).

THE COVENANT "GOAL"

After years of suffering during the Babylonian Captivity, the judgment on Israel's false loyalties, there emerged one of the loftiest revelations of the meaning of the Covenant. In the fifty-third chapter of Isaiah appears the portrait of the "Suffering Servant." Speaking for all mankind, it is written: "All we like sheep have gone astray; we have turned every one to his own way; and the Lord has laid on him the iniquity of us all." Here Israel began to see in its own history the history of mankind—that of rebellion, arrogance, self-elevation to divinity.

But who is the "him" on whom the punishment has fallen? This is not to ask who best fulfills this role, but of whom was Isaiah himself thinking? Most likely Israel herself. No longer is Israel's Covenant calling to be understood as a call to splendor, but to humiliation, not to world acclaim, but to rejection, not to power, but to humble sorrow and grief. Israel was not the goal of the Covenant but its means. Through this suffering that was more than Israel deserved, mankind as such would be brought to repentance whereby the Divine covenantal destiny for *all* men could be perceived.

Isaiah's writings rise to magnificent heights as he

feels for words to express this vision of the kingdom of God, the final transformation of earth as the ultimate completion of God's Covenant plans. This is a vision of the Divine-human venture whose precise nature can be known only as the Divine-human activity is worked out in freedom throughout the processes of history (Isaiah 2:1-4; 11:6-9; Jeremiah 31:31-34). Never is the end in doubt, nor the faithfulness of God questioned. *The* problem is man's response, for Israel's history is the microscopic record of man as such. Through Israel was God's Will becoming known, but in Israel is man's rebellion against God personified. This is the paradox of existence recorded in the Bible as the central fact of human history.

THE PATTERN OF HISTORY

The unifying question of biblical history was the question, What does Israel's past say in this moment as to the meaning of both present and future? The one answer was the living reality of the Covenant relation. Through their own experience came the testimony that in faithfulness to God comes meaning and the fullness of life; in rebellion against God comes inevitable ruin of self and society. Contemporary historians such as Herbert Butterfield have seen something of this truth in concluding that the one recognizable pattern in history is the inevitable judgment on the immoralities of nations.

It was from this encompassing faith-perspective that the Hebrews viewed creation. In editing Genesis, the explanatory legends, the "scientific" myths, the prehistoric records were brought together, but no longer were they for the purpose of describing how creation came into being or for explaining the order in which the various cosmic ingredients emerged. The orienting perspective for the editorial rewriting of this material was the religious question of why, of ultimate meaning: not how did God create the world, but why; not how does it operate, but what does it mean.

Into this ancient material the Hebraic writers breathed the truth of the God-man relation gleaned from countless years' experience. In the myth of Adam and Eve we find a living story that is no longer primarily the causal explanation of human sin and the rebelliousness of creation, but a revelation of the ultimate meaning of human activity and the purpose behind the enigma of creation. Immersing himself in the faith-perspective of Genesis, Kierkegaard has wisely said: "How man fell, I admit I do not know; why man fell, I now know within my own self."

In the form of an original human couple, Israel incarnated its profound knowledge of God's intention for man, and man's repeated response to this Divine Call. This living story is often turned into a sterile theological doctrine of original sin, in which the act of Adam and Eve is made into the explanatory cause of man's universal selfishness through which men are damned. The writers of the Old Testament, however, took no such view. This original account was a *living* portrait revealing in depth the human response that re-occurred time after time as Israel rejected her Cove-nant God for self-gain, reaping the destructive consequences.

This repetition of the "fall" is portrayed innumera-ble times in the minor incidents of Israel's life, as, for example, in the accounts of the tower of Babel, and the ark and flood. These accounts reflect the fundamental biblical insistence that the ebb and flow of Hebraic history is structured by the same cycle. The call to Covenant through Abraham leads through human re-sponse to bondage in Egypt. The exodus from Egypt is understood by the Israelites as the *new* creation by God, yet through human rebellion its eventual end is the Babylonian Captivity. God's creative act of the "second exodus" is a re-creation which restores Israel to the promised land, and once again man's faithless-ness negates the Divine Act by reducing living faith to sterile legalism.

In Jesus Christ there occurs God's supreme act. Al-though here too man seeks to negate God through murder, the resurrection is God's eternal victory over all human rebellion. Through it forgiveness and resto-

ration are offered to all those who accept this supreme
Divine Act. The stories of creation and fall must be
understood from this perspective of living, ongoing
history in which the past is seen as type and archetype
for revealing the abiding truth of the present. This
pattern of history religiously understood by the Hebrew is not unlike the secular observation of Henry
Miller in our own time: "Once every thousand years
stillness fades into a shape that men may crucify."

CREATION FOR COVENANT

The Israelites understood God's original act of creation not as an explanation of how things came into being, but as a revelation of God's intention *for* creation.
Why did God create? This is *the* question, and the
biblical answer is clear—creation is for Covenant. God
created the entire cosmic process in order to enter into
Covenant with man for bringing creation to completion.

In the creation account of Genesis we have revealed
three fundamental ingredients of the Hebraic faith.
First, all that is is created by God; therefore it is good
and according to his Divine Purpose. Second, man is
created to do God's Will in a cosmic enterprise which
He has willed to be a Divine-human adventure. Third,
man is free, within limits, to respond positively *or* neg-
atively to this Divine Invitation.

It is within these basic affirmations that the Jew and the Christian attempt to explore history in the present to discover God's Will. This is to be oriented toward a Divine open-ended future that is increasingly revealed in every reoccurring present.

CREATION FOR INCARNATION

For the Christian, however, God's revelation of his Will for man did not end with the fall of the Jewish nation. Rather, this collapse marked the signaling of a great spiritualization of man's understanding of the Divine covenantal Will, a spiritualization through which the Divine-human relation was elevated to even greater heights than before. God's covenantal relation is no longer promise, but concrete, historical fact. In Jesus Christ, God and man have entered a oneness of flesh in such a way that the Will of God for all time and space became incarnated in time and space. In this figure, the suffering servant was so completely realized that from that time forth God's Will in the present finds the instrument for its discovery in the birth, life, death, and resurrection of the Divine Will Incarnate.

About how this impossible possibility can be, we shall concern ourselves later. At this point it is sufficient to see that for the Christian this is the completing act of Creation. Creation is understood as having occurred for the sake of this one act, for in it creation receives

its vindication in meaning, evil receives its supreme
theodicy in the covenantal suffering of God himself,
and cosmic meaning is guaranteed and brought into
being. In Christ, Divine Purpose and human response
become one in such a manner that God's intention for
all creation is revealed. From this point in history,
meaning is measured in terms of the achievement of the
creative wholeness incarnated in Jesus Christ. In one
sense, the Incarnation is a new revelation; yet in another sense it is the completion of all that had been
revealed over the centuries of the Divine-human experience recorded in the Old Testament. Christ came
in "the fullness of time," when the Jews had been prepared in terms of experience, discipline, language, and
concept to understand in sufficient part the final revelation of God's intent for creation.

Consequently, in understanding creation the Christian does not begin with some supposed literal tran-
scription of a primitive biblical eyewitness, but begins
with the fullness of creation, Jesus Christ. From this
faith-perspective he proceeds backwards to an understanding of the meaning of God's "original" act, ir-
respective of how or when it may have occurred. This
too was the method of the ancient Hebrew, for the
meaning of creation was revealed to him only from the
perspective of the Covenant relation. Consequently,
from the perspective of the Christian's understanding
of ultimate meaning, creation can be understood in no

other way than as "Creation through Covenant for Incarnation."

Myth and the Problem of Man

It is from this general perspective that we must attempt to understand the over-all meaning of the Christian world-view as it enters into dialogue with the present human dilemma. After centuries of regarding the question of man as basically solved, we in our time are coming to see that a central problem of our age is, "Who *is* man?" We are being forced to admit that we do not know.

The nineteenth century saw man as essentially noble, as rational, as structured with an innate moral law, oriented by a love of community and an ability for infinite perfection and progress. But as man in our decade soars through space and has the planets within his sights, the world from which he blasts off still shudders before the indictments of Buchenwald and Auschwitz, and the promise of a nuclear holocaust.

Nineteenth-century religion followed the same general spirit. Optimism swept away such "archaic" religious ideas as original sin and the fall as neither true nor possible, eliminating in like manner such ideas as salvation and redemption as irrelevant and unnecessary. The Golden Rule replaced the Cross, and education rather than conversion became the vehicle to religious faith. Jesus was seen not as the God-man, but as the perfect man, as an outstanding teacher, as the finest example of moral behavior. But now, after encountering the demonic exposed in our age by the inhumanity of man to man, such liberal Christianity appears as empty, hollow, and irrelevant as the other platitudes bequeathed to us by the nineteenth century. If Christianity is to become meaningful and relevant, it must face up to man's dilemma—his own self —and provide an answer that is unique and redemptive.

As contemporary Christian thinkers have reflected upon the nature of man, there has come the awareness that the ancient doctrines that have been discarded are the most meaningful categories possible for bringing insight to man's dilemma. Most important of all are the ideas of "creation" and the "fall." After centuries in which no first-rate intellectual was willing to speak of the "fall," it is significant that this category is fast becoming indispensable.

The name Adam can literally mean two things: "first man" or "every man." Adam has often been understood in Christian circles in the first sense. Consequently, because of his disobedience, Adam was punished by God, and his offspring cursed to the end of time. In a scientific age such as ours, however, something of the Hebraic meaning is returning. The story is coming to be regarded not as history, but as "myth." Myth here in no way means falsehood or fabrication.

Plato's creation of myth in the *Timaeus* is quite illuminating. When Plato came to the problem of the
origin of the world, he insisted that Plato the philosopher must give way to Plato the poet. In matters so
deep, man cannot understand with clear logic; he
must feel the truth through symbols. One can only
point toward the ultimate truth, not comprehend such
truth in a rational system.

It is in this spirit that the story of Adam and Eve
must be read. It is when we read it as the portrait of
every man that we arrive at a profound analysis of the
real nature of the human dilemma. What Adam did,
we all do, but not because he did it. Rather, the very
motives in Adam's act are ours. We see in Adam, as
did the ancient Jew, a disturbingly penetrating self-
portrait. Here is revealed ourselves and our history. As
Adam was Israel, so Adam is I.

CREATION AND THE POSSIBILITY OF FALLENNESS

The cosmic framework for the Adamic myth appears in the first four words of Scripture: "In the
beginning, God. . . ." For the Hebrew, God alone is
self-constituted, self-sustained. Of Him alone can it
be truly said, HE IS (Exodus 3:14; Isaiah 43:10). Of
all else, one must say that it is "becoming," that it has
not attained fullness of being but is in the process of
striving toward it. To see the world and everything in

it in this contingent fashion is to know that God alone is perfect and eternal, dependent upon nothing and in need of nothing to explain either his existence or his nature. Of God alone can we say that his essence is to exist.

Of all else we must say that its existence is not necessary, that it is because He is, that it is contingent. In a word, man is a "creature." He is a creature, however, not because he is fallen or defective, but because he is dependent in every moment upon the Creator for his existence. This is what it means to say that God created from nothing: before God acted, He alone was.

Because God is the fullness of being, everything which he creates is also good insofar as it exists at all. It is here that we come to the central point witnessed to in Genesis: though everything that God creates is positively good, it is not incorruptibly or unchangeably good. God alone is unchanging, for he alone is uncreated, eternal, self-dependent. But man, being created out of nonbeing, as it were, would disappear into nonbeing, into nothingness, if it were not for the continuous creative power of God.

It is because man is created that man is able to become imperfect, for though his existence is good, he has a potentiality for nonbeing. If this contingent being strives for total liberty, for autonomy, by rejecting God, then imperfection comes into the universe. To do this is for man to become a living self-contradiction, for whether he knows it or not, he is striving for death, striving to be what he is not. He is sawing off the limb on which he sits. If he were ever to achieve such independence, he would by this very achievement become nonexistent. Anything other than God cannot be God, for all but God, by its very nature, is created and thus dependent.

LOVE AND THE "NECESSITY" OF FREEDOM

This possibility of created being affirming nonbeing, of frustrating God's good act of creation by becoming an existing self-contradiction, is possible only if this power is given to man by God. It is precisely at this point that the problem of evil arises. As Dostoevsky's Ivan cries out, if human freedom is given at the price of suffering children on the ends of Turkish spears, we must hand back the ticket to God's world. Archibald MacLeish in our own time put it this way: Why does God permit man the freedom to wreak evil upon his fellow men; can God escape responsibility for this without being revealed as either a malevolent or impotent Deity?

The Christian answer to such searching questions resides in understanding God's purpose in creating the world. Since God is perfect being, he has no need of anything. There is no way in which God can fulfill his nature further by creating. God's motive for creating must then be other than God. It is in Jesus Christ that the supreme Will of God for creation is revealed. In creating for Incarnation, God reveals that he has created for *agape*, for love of a very special type. Love as man now knows it is *eros*, the love of an object because it is of value to the self. One loves a car or a woman because these are of value to him, and the intensity of this love is determined by their ability to satisfy one's own desires. *Eros* love is impossible for God, for he has no need of anything.

Consequently, the love through which and for which God creates is *agape*, selfless love. God loves, not for his own sake, but for the sake of that which is loved. The greatest thing which God can create is a creature capable of the highest form of existence possible—the life of *agape*, that which is supremely Godlike. That this is precisely what God did in creation is the heart of the Christian revelation through the Incarnation: *God created out of love for love*. Only in achieving this love for which he by his very nature was created does man come to fullness, to completion—to Godlikeness. Man, Genesis affirms, was created in the *imago Dei*, the image of God. In the Incarnation God's image is revealed: it is the capacity for *agape*, for self-giving love (Ephesians 3:14-19).

It is here that we reach the crucial point for understanding God's gift of freedom and man's capacity for evil. Love to be love must be free. Just as is the case in

God's loving act of creation, love cannot be a necessary act. Necessary or coerced love is no longer love. Love, by definition, is free, spontaneous; love must be willed; it must be an expression of one's own self; it must be chosen from alternatives. The possibility of God creating loving automatons is ruled out by definition, for such as these cannot love but only obey, and even the word obey does not really fit. Consequently, if the goal of creation is *agape*, God has no option but to grant man the gift of freedom. Out of love, for love, God creates man free, free to affirm his Creator and his neighbor in love, or free to reject this entire cosmic purpose. This is the *risk* which God must take if he is to achieve his purpose of love. *And God took it.*

MAN AS THE JUNCTURE OF CREATION

As a consequence of his existence in freedom, man stands in the most strategic position in all creation. He alone of all creatures has both freedom and the reason necessary to use this freedom creatively. Thus far in God's plan, everything in creation is good, and there is nothing evil whatsoever. As we have indicated, the only way in which evil can enter the world is if nonbeing becomes affirmed as being, if falsification is affirmed as being truth. Inanimate things such as plants and animals cannot do this, for they can affirm nothing; they are simply as they are, without freedom. In this world, only man has the capacity to bring evil into the world.

Genesis records that "on the seventh day," the "day" in which we now live, God rests, and man's task of tending the "garden" of the world begins. The completion of creation is to be the Divine-human venture that we call history. With love as the motive and goal of creation, it could not be otherwise; human response is the indispensable completion of Divine Creativity. Love entails offer and response. It is the expression of God's majesty as well as his omnipotence that he who is all, graciously limits himself that creation may be a Divine-human partnership. This is the central affirmation of the Covenant relation fulfilled in the Incarnation: God entering the human domain as lover, as friend, as participant, as partner.

This central idea can be understood only through a careful analysis of the possibilities presented by God's creation of man for love through freedom. Reinhold Niebuhr, following Kierkegaard's lead, speaks of this Divine intent as a placing of man at the juncture of nature and spirit, or of finitude and freedom. Man clearly belongs to the realm of nature—he is finite. He is composed of drives, needs, instincts, and passions, craving fulfillment, just as the other animals are. All that the biologist tells us about man in terms of the evolutionary process is relevant, and no understanding of the

human specie has any hope of success if these animal-
istic aspects are neglected or minimized.

Yet as soon as this is said, one is driven to affirm
more. Man is a *unique* animal; he is indeed "lord of
creation." Man has a more developed brain, and it
would seem that his superiority has something to do
with this fact. But in what sense does mental capacity
give an ability not possessed by other animals? The answer for the Christian resides in understanding freedom, for it is the foundation of the human capacity for
love, for morality, for responsibility, and for creative
response. Human freedom is rooted in man's capacity
for self-consciousness, for what can be called self-
transcendence. Man alone has the capacity to make an
object out of himself. One can reflect back upon an
incident that happened to him in the past. He can see
the situation as though it were going on now, and in-
trospect: "Why on earth did I ever do that—look at
the spectacle I really made—there I am, in the middle
of the room, thinking myself the life of the party—but
just see how I really looked in the eyes of others—what
an idiot!"

What, in effect, one is able to do through such a
process of self-transcendence is to come to some degree of objectivity about himself. He rises above himself and sees himself, at least in part, as others see him.
If we look carefully, we can see that the "principle"
which the mind is using in such self-judgment is actu-

ally the "golden rule"—"do unto others as you would have them do unto you." This principle we use constantly in our evaluations of others. We see the ridiculous portrait they cut, the way they strut, the false self-assurance they display, the self-aggrandizement with which they are permeated, the phoniness of the pretenses that they believe are so convincing. We see all this clearly, for we see the person naked, as it were. And our judgment is simply this: what we are recognizing is the degree to which they act toward others in a way that they would never permit another to act toward them. Kant was not far from the mark in seeing self-consistency as the nature of natural morality.

The degree to which I transcend myself, see myself as though I were another person acting toward me, to that degree do I stand in a position to evaluate similarly my own actions. I can offend myself, just as I would be offended if a stranger had done the same thing to me. Conscience is, as it were, the words of the prophet Nathan spoken to David, appearing silently over the honest portraits of memory and imagination—"Thou art the man."

Despite this sacred ability that characterizes man, it is a disturbing but undeniable fact that man tries in every manner possible to keep from viewing himself from this self-transcendent perspective, for it cuts him down to size. When in those special moments we are forced to transcend ourselves, to become self-conscious, we inevitably "pull our punches." We regard our portrait in a far more pleasing light than we deserve.

But as hard as we try, we can never quite remain content in our self-deception. Man's nature is not so simple. Man's capacity is to transcend himself infinitely. Not only can I reflect upon myself, but I can reflect upon myself reflecting upon myself, and then again reflect upon myself reflecting upon myself reflecting upon myself, *ad infinitum.* I can keep catching myself prejudicing my case, and thereby purify my self-perspective as I increasingly see myself as others see me. More and more is it possible for me to stand in a position to act toward others as I would have them act toward me, that is, in love.

It is in this capacity that human freedom resides, for not only can the self reflect upon its past, but upon its present and future as well. To the degree that man's self-transcendent capacity is employed, to that degree can future possibilities be viewed as present happenings, and evaluated in terms of their consequences. In this way basic needs can be modified: one can compensate, sublimate, subordinate, regulate, and sometimes even negate them, in terms of the ideals, goals, and "oughts" gained through self-transcendence.

As man envisages consequences in advance, channeling and regulating present drives in terms of future possibilities, he is liberated from his natural level and freed for the development of his higher capacities. Many a person becomes involved in sexual trouble and afterward says, "If I had only known." Through self-transcendence, one can know both self and future possibilities; he can seek to avoid those situations in which particular natural instincts can effect their powerful "determinism."

CREATURELINESS AND ANXIETY

These are the basic dimensions of man's nature for which Adam stands as eternal portrait. It is the consistent biblical witness that the body is not evil; man's instincts are God-given and God-intended. Consequently, the struggle which is life, the venture which comes from being at the juncture of nature and spirit, is God-intended and *in no way* a sign of fallenness. To stand at this juncture is simply to be finite, and finitude is good.

The result, psychologically, of being at this juncture is a state best indicated by the word "anxiety." Anxiety comes primarily from this fact that although man is natural, in transcending himself these animal drives can be transformed into spiritual qualities. There is no limit to this transformation. In fact, the higher one's attainment, the more sensitive he becomes to the greater potentialities yet remaining. Man is inevitably anxious, for he never fully realizes what he has within himself and his culture to become.

This capacity for transformation can be illustrated well in terms of the sexual capacity. Every person has a sexual drive that must be satisfied in some manner, or, as Freud has made clear, frustration and psychological disorderings will result. Such disorderings never occur in the purely animal realm, for when sexual passion arises, the animal satisfies it quickly and directly without other factors tempering the satisfaction. The animal can be satisfied simply by release of passion. Simple release of a bothersome drive, however, can never really satisfy man, for the possibilities that sex presents are tremendously elevated by his ability for self-transcendence. Through such an ability, sex can become a transforming act between a couple who in marriage have pledged themselves to becoming one flesh, fulfilling the spiritual, emotional, and physical needs of each other without thought of self. Through the sex act these two incomplete beings find their other selves and are completed, time after time being restored symbolically and actually in mutual fulfillment in the oneness that is love. Sex becomes an event both of pledge and realization in which the total man and the total woman are transformed in a relationship that elevates the purely natural to one of the highest spiritual acts of which man is capable, for which, Scripture affirms, the only proper analogy is the love of God for man. The sexual passion presents unlimited possibilities beginning with lust and ending in the heights of pure love. For man, standing in the middle, the threat of guilt is ever present. Anything less than this transforming spirituality leaves man anxious and painfully aware of his unfulfilled potentialities.

Such expressions of anxiety we could call "moral," but anxiety has other forms. A second form might well be called "physical." Man, as a natural being, belongs to the physical cycle of birth and death. All that is physical is limited by time. For the purely natural creature, his inevitable end is not known, and the process is "natural." With the capacity for self-transcendence, however, comes the awareness of uncertainty in all things. No man is totally unaware of the complete loss of self entailed by death, even if his feel for this fact is only instinctual. He is painfully aware of the gradual disappearance all around him of friends, security, vitality, and the like. Death and life are incompatibles, but man stands at the juncture of them.

But, though death is the absolute threat, it is witnessed to in many immediate ways. We are contingent beings in the historical sense, for we live in just this speck of history, and are shackled by its perspective, problems, goals, and illusions. As Tillich has said, we begin "in a contingent moment, ending in a contingent moment, filled with experiences which are themselves contingent with respect to quality and quantity."

Likewise, man is conscious of being spatially bound. We are determined in religion, politics, economics, ideals, habits, by the geographical spot of our origin. I must live the ambiguity of knowing myself determined spatially and temporally, and also knowing that I could be quite different. I seem to be determined to be what I am, but there seems to be no ultimate necessity behind it all.

The anxiety involved in such physical ambiguities inevitably accompanies man's freedom, even though this freedom may well be the means for ultimate meaning.

Anxiety has still a third type which we could call "spiritual." An animal is totally determined in the pattern of its life. As a natural being, man has within him such a pattern. As a self-transcending being, however, he can transform such necessity by setting goals, ideals, and principles for himself. It is for man alone to know that mere existence is not self-justifying, is not in itself sufficient reason for continuing. Man alone can know the gnawing feeling of emptiness, the haunting possibility that all may be ultimately meaningless. Man alone is able to ask WHY because he alone is free; but he is free only because, in some sense, he is separated from the meaning which he needs.

Because of all these factors, doubt is a problem implied by man's very existence. Existence in self-transcendence is existence in freedom; existence in freedom

is living the life of risk. This is the state that is anxiety.
This ambiguity, this anxiety, which comes from living
at the juncture was conveyed well by the statement re-
cently of a teen-ager: "I would like to be in the same
moment an earthworm and a rider to the moon."

ANXIETY AND CREATIVITY

Thus far we have been concerned to understand the
nature of anxiety. Our task now is to understand the
positive dimensions of anxiety which make it a necessary condition for the fulfillment of the Divine Plan.
Man was created to accept anxiety positively, for it is
the precondition of human creativity. The human task
is to stand at the juncture of nature and spirit, creatively transforming the natural in freedom through
this self-transcendent capacity. This is the Divine-human enterprise for completing the finite as the covenantal kingdom of God, the ideal community of
reciprocal love in which each regards his neighbor as
he regards himself. This is the condition of faith for
which man was created: free acceptance of creation
and man's place within it, based on the trust that finitude is God-intended, that in man's oneness of will
with the Divine Will the creative possibilities of every
"now" will be disclosed and increasingly realized.

For a creature to have freedom, creation cannot be
complete. Knowledge cannot be certain, moral effort

cannot be determined, nature must have unrealized
possibilities, meaning cannot be guaranteed, history
must be open-ended—man must stand in the situation
of anxiety. Love, creativity: these are impossibilities
without the tension between "is" and "ought," between "was" and "might have been," between "actuality" and "potentiality," between "ugliness" and
"beauty," between "sin" and "faith." Anxiety is for
the creativity which is love.

"Fall" as Escapism

In this God-created process, rich with radiant possibility, stands man, every man, at the juncture. As in
Adam, so in every man—man rebels, and though rebellion is in no way necessary, it appears from the
record of history to be inevitable. Man does not trust
God, but relies on himself; he insists on being not a
creature of faith but of sight. He attempts to deal with
the problem of anxiety himself, without God. To do
this, however, is to render anxiety negative rather than
positive. Anxiety, rather than being the precondition
of creativity, now becomes the precondition of sin. If
God is not accepted as the center of one's life, anxiety
cannot be dealt with effectively. Anxiety can no longer
be regarded as the means to anything of value; it can
be seen only as a highly undesirable condition to be es-
caped at all costs. Since man, in denying God, thereby

denies ultimate meaning *in* the juncture, his only possibility is to try to give himself finite meaning by
escaping the juncture.

Escapism as Pride

There are only two possibilities open for man if he
is to reject God's intended place for him in creation.
Since anxiety is the result of a juncture, one can seek
to escape it only by pretending away one or the other
of the dimensions making up this juncture.

The first attempt is the way of false pride or arrogance. Man comes to regard his self-transcendence as
revealing actual rather than potential states of his own
being. For the man of faith, the natural and spiritual
are always in transforming dialogue, in creative tension; self-transcendence reveals possibilities that creatively judge one's present attainments by exhibiting
the potentialities resident in all things. In the sin of
pride, however, one sees something of his self-transcendent possibilities, but denies or greatly minimizes
his unrealized natural aspects. He attempts to convince
himself that there is no real tension between his possibilities and his attainments. What he ought to be is
what he talks himself into thinking he is. In effect, his
self-transcendence becomes a façade for hiding weak-
ness and inadequacy.

One rises only to the first level of self-transcendence;

he chooses not to reflect upon himself reflecting upon himself. He sees in himself or his family or his group or his party or his nation or his cause only what he wishes to see, using his self-transcendence only for the purpose of self-congratulation, self-aggrandizement, and, in the end, self-deception. He elevates himself out of all perspective, judging all things definitively in terms of *his* morality, *his* spirituality, *his* ideas, *his* perspective. The self thus becomes the end-all and be-all of one's activities and thoughts.

From one's birth on, this tendency is present. Man by his physical nature sees the world through his own eyes. The sun and stars revolve around him, and when he sleeps, everything else sleeps. If he is not present when a tree falls, then, as far as he is concerned, no tree fell. The transition is subtle until a physical characteristic which promises infinite transformation becomes, instead, a way of life. I am white; white is best. I am Methodist; Methodism is final. I am a man; there is nothing higher. Such is the irrationality of false pride. Put in biblical language, this is the attempt by man to become God. Anxiety reveals man to be finite and not infinite, man and not God. Anxiety brings judgment; therefore anxiety must be "eliminated" if man is even to begin this pretense toward Godhood. Anxiety brings tremendous challenge and possibilities for creativity; therefore it must be "eliminated" if man is to escape the responsibility of living.

Escapism as Sensuality

The second way in which man can attempt to escape anxiety is through sensuality or libertinism. In a way, it is the opposite response to the way of pride. It is the attempt to see one's self only as a natural being; it is a pretending away of one's capacities for self-transcendence. In effect, it is to act as though one had no capacity for freedom—"I was born in Brooklyn; what more can you expect?"

In the end, however, both these responses are characterized by arrogance, by conceit, by self-aggrandizement. The attempt in both cases is to make one's own self supreme by affirming only one dimension of man. The sensualist, too, is saying, All that really matters is the alleviation of *my* needs. This, in its own way, is pride, for it implies that I alone am an "end," and all else is a "means."

It is only through such a Christian understanding of man that the basic problems of man's interrelations receive illuminating foundation. Man is a social creature whose natural love of company makes human fulfillment possible. But such a positive capacity stands also through human freedom to be an instrument of destruction. Each man's attempts at self-deception are never fully successful, for always in the quiet moment, or in the eyes of another living being, the truth about one's self cannot remain shut out. But what a man cannot do by himself becomes far easier in the company of like weaknesses seeking like deception. The arrogance that one would never even dream of perpetrating by himself becomes expected behavior in a mob, or made into formal creeds in the most sophisticated groups. We can comfortably see this best in the examples all around us of the underprivileged group or the undeveloped nation suddenly given its freedom. But if we dare look at matters honestly instead of in terms of blacks and whites, we could instructively find illustrations of the biblical truth in labor-management tensions, Church and state conflicts, race relations, and the chaos of international affairs. All these are problems rooted ultimately in the nature of man, and pride is the term which best ferrets out the real problem.

ADAM AS EVERY MAN

This is the affirmation of Genesis—that Adam and Eve, instead of acknowledging freely and fully that both their existence and their good come solely from God, affirm for themselves the self-sufficiency which by nature belongs only to God. The best phrase to point to the quality of their act is "the arrogance of ingratitude." Instead of freely accepting in thankfulness all the gifts of infinite love issuing in creation, they desire one thing more—to pretend that all things come from themselves alone, that they are second to none. Through their own bloated egos they crave to be utterly autonomous. "Eat," says the serpent, "and ye shall be as God!" This is sin—the attempt to sever by living denial the relation between God and man on which one's very existence depends. It is in breaking this relation that selfishness, hatred, greed, and murder come into being, for God's Will is being rejected for self-will. He who seeks to be God, in not being divine, becomes less than human. In politics or in the self, there is no doubting Lord Acton's words: "Power tends to corrupt; absolute power corrupts absolutely."

THE FALL OF CREATION

In essence, then, sin is the act of professing nonbeing to be being, to act as though the nonexistent were existent. When man professes to be of the same status as the Creator, a self-sufficient source of good, then the creature is living a lie, is affirming a metaphysical untruth to be the basic truth. He lives his life on the basis of a supposed truth which if true would mean man's total extinction. Man is affirming something other than God to be god, and in so doing is permitting nonbeing to become effective.

With this act, evil enters the world, not as being, which would be a contradiction, but as an effective power in the lives of men. Nonbeing becomes evil when a free creature gives to it in his life the status of ultimate being. It is when man says, "Let my own self be my god," that nonbeing becomes a power, for it is the pledge, conscious or unconscious, that the undoing of God's good for man is the aim of one's life. This in no way means that self, money, success, or pleasure are evil in themselves, for they are God-intended. But when they become the end-all of one's life, then man has brought evil into being by making a good destructive.

The consequences of human rebellion, as Genesis mythologically reveals, is the turning of creation against man as though in vengeance for the bondage into which man has cast her. That is, no longer is the relation between man and creation creative, for no longer does man stand in the power of God to undertake the completion of nature entailed by the covenantal relation of creation. As man attempts to escape anxiety through self-aggrandizement, his motivation becomes not that of fulfilling and completing creation, but the desire to exploit it for his own selfish advantage. As we are seeing powerfully in our generation, the exploited turns in vengeance, and the positive, creative tension posed by creation becomes the destructive threat to autonomous human life, to man's self-imposed meaning and purpose.

If human creativity is to be possible, if history is to be a Divine-human venture, creation must be incomplete. Through trust, faith, man stands with God as co-creator; the incompleteness of creation is not an evil incompleteness, but the condition for love. It is not an end but a means. If, however, man declares himself to be god, then an incomplete creation becomes an end, a threat standing indifferently over against "autonomous" man. For a creature of the fall, creation is fallen.

GRACE IN CREATION

Although man's rebellion logically entails man's non-existence, all is not lost, for God continues to sustain man in his rebellion. This is the dark side of grace, for although the enigma of creation cannot in itself bring man into the creative dialogue which is faith, it can become positive in its negativity if acknowledged as the consequence of man's rebellion; in this manner man can be humbled to the true God-man relation of creation, to the prerequisite for the faith that redeems.

Augustine points perceptively to the grace in creation with his celebrated confession, "O Lord, Thou hast made us for Thyself, and we are restless until we find our rest in Thee." That is, we are so created that peace, fullness, and meaning are possible only through supreme devotion to the God who has structured us in existence. Our despair, frustration, and experiences of meaninglessness in rejecting God for "idols" are really an expression of this negative grace. It is to our age most especially that Pascal's words of faith can bring light: "I would not have found Thee, had Thou not first sought me out, frustrating all my ways."

THE SATANIC

Yet what are we to make of the Satanic? This idea appears only occasionally in Scripture. When it does appear, however, Satan, though God's adversary, is always subordinate to God. It is most in harmony with the biblical world-view to conceive Satan as the incarnation of the possibility of evil resident within man's capacity for freedom. The Satanic possibility cannot be removed without destroying freedom. If God, in effect, had said to man, "You are free to do whatever I want you to do," freedom would be negated. A child in a locked room with only one toy is not free; only in the presence of lamps and vases, too, with the command "Thou shalt not touch," does the child possess freedom and the means for discovering its meaning. There can be no freedom without the forbidden fruit, which stands for the possibility of rebellion, and the Satanic temptation, which stands for the organic demonism of rebellion as it infiltrates all things through cumulative power, prestige, and influence. To destroy the possibility of the Satanic would be to destroy freedom and thereby to destroy love as the God-intended goal of creation.

AN ANSWER TO EVIL

What we have said is really the thrust of Dostoevsky's final answer to the atheistic taunts of his own Ivan. Ivan had said, just as two and two are four, so if God permits human suffering and evil, God is not God. This is all that the Euclidean mind sees, intent as it is, in Ivan's own words, "not to understand, but to stick to the facts." If the suffering of children is the price man has to pay for freedom, Ivan will hand back the ticket—God cannot be God.

Dostoevsky came to see, however, that there is another way of regarding the problem posed by creation, a way gained not through reason but, as with the Israelites, through experience. Only when one experiences his own self as the cause of the sufferings of others, and experiences through such suffering the humbling blow through which love is born, only then is he in any position to ask whether God's permission of freedom is worth the risk. Only in this way can one come to see for himself that if the suffering of the innocent few is the necessary price for the possibility of the fulfillment of mankind in love, then *God can be God only if he permits such freedom, even at that price*. One cannot say that God is truly the God of love if, for the sake of the possibility of a suffering child, he robs *all* mankind, like the Grand Inquisitor, of the very capability—his freedom for love—that makes man more than an animal, more than a rock or an automaton, or more than a number in an ant heap.

THE FALL AND HUMAN IMPOTENCE

To understand God's Incarnate Activity as Redeemer, it is necessary that we see clearly the condition of man created by human rebellion. The fulfillment of life is *agape;* the frustration of life is *eros.* *Agape* is loving as one has been loved—without regard for self. But when a man acts as though *his* reason, *his* desires, *his* power, are supreme over those of God his true good, then in such pride the total orientation, the total love of his life, becomes the self. Inevitably, everything else is held to be of value only insofar as it fulfills his own wants. This becomes true even of one's worship of God, if one still admits him to exist.

This perversion that occurs is not caused by one's nature; it is a perversion rooted in one's own will. Psychologically, one finds himself in a situation from which there would seem to be no escape. Even if one now decides to seek his true end, selfless love, he can only be motivated to do so by a self-*ish* love, thereby undermining the whole struggle. The will seeks *agape* only if it is convinced that such love will satisfy its desires better. Thus the stronger the motivation for love, the further the will drives itself from it. Once a man chooses to live as though he were God, in not being God such a choice makes him less than a man. He has perverted and dissipated the power of the *imago dei*—the power of freedom to choose *agape*, to render anxiety creative.

THE DRAMA OF HISTORY

It is the witness of Scripture that throughout the history of Israel, God has acted dramatically to bring man to an awareness of the lie on the basis of which he is living, recalling him repeatedly to the Covenant relation. Yet God's activity is limited by his sublime goals for man, for his goals require human freedom. God cannot coerce human response without destroying his very purpose for creating. Consequently, it is through what Scripture calls "God's mighty acts in history" that God attempts to restore man to the new relation of forgiveness, of redemption. It is by dramatic event that God attempts to evoke human self-consciousness. Time after time, as it were, the situation of a new Eden is created, and time after time the fall is re-enacted.

For the Christian, this mode of Divine Activity is the work of Christ, the Son. That is, this Divine Activity of redemption operating throughout history became fully offered and revealed in the Incarnation, when man had rejected or remained oblivious to all other Divine Offers of love. The subject matter of biblical history is God's righteous Will and yet his continuing mercy to love.

It is this redemptive activity of God that makes a drama of history, that makes of time more than the unraveling of man's self-inflicted fate. Upon discovering the sin of Adam and Eve, God is portrayed as removing the rough leaves of the fig tree with which they had clothed themselves, giving them soft garments of fur. From the very beginning, love tempers justice in God's dealings. Still each new generation re-enacts and continues the fall by new acts of selfish pride. Cain, the son of Adam, killed his brother Abel in a fit of jealousy, and the new corruption began again. By act after act the pattern of rebellion was set.

As a "last" resort, Noah and his family were made the instruments of a new beginning; by dramatic event the freedom of Eden was renewed. Yet once again, man chooses to be his own god, portrayed this time in the attempt to build the tower of Babel by which to storm heaven. Man purchases rebellion with his freedom, but the real price is the forfeiture of fulfillment in and through love.

And so God begins the third act in the Divine-human drama: he elects through Abraham a special people as the Covenant agents of his redemptive work in history. Yet even honor such as this proved no match for human arrogance. Israel lost faith in this Covenant relation, and in its dissipation fell slaves to Egypt.

When Israel had experienced the choices of her freedom, Moses is called forth, chosen to offer a new land
in which the redemptive community of love could be
brought into being.

Throughout Scripture, the portrait which is given
of man's response is damning to the reader. So here.
With shouts and song and joy in liberation, the people
march forth from Egypt, confident in their trust for
Moses, truly the Lord's appointed. Upon encountering the very first obstacle, however, their shouts are
these:

> "Is it because there are no graves in Egypt that you
> have taken us away to die in the wilderness? What have
> you done to us in bringing us out of Egypt? Is not this
> what we said to you in Egypt, 'Let us alone and let us
> serve the Egyptians'?" (Exodus 14:11-12)

Nevertheless, God delivers them through his mighty
act at the Red Sea. But even as Moses is in the moun-
tains receiving the Ten Commandments of the Covenant from God, Israel in the valley doubts, and in its
doubting molds idols to animal gods. On and on,
throughout the history of Israel, goes this abiding motif of Divine Restoration and human rebellion.

INCARNATION AS THE CENTER OF HISTORY

And so, we read, God does the most that love can
do: to present his love so fully that its impact may

negate the power of rebellion once and for all, restoring man to the freedom in which the Adamic choice is again presented. But now the choice offered to man is a choice with the experience of evil and suffering engraved on his mind, and a revelation before him of God's very Being as utter and complete *agape*, thereby exposing the full calling which freedom entails. As a result, what is here made possible is no restoration to the naïve innocence of Eden; history cannot be negated, for it lives within our very beings. What is being offered is a new creation, for through the Incarnation of God himself in the man Jesus emerges the total revelation of both God and man. This convergence of human knowledge and Divine Love is the center point of all history.

This revelation occurs in such a way that not only can man's indifference be shaken by the dramatic intensity of the event, by its completeness, indeed, by its thoroughgoing human-ness, but it is done in such a way that the moral structure of God and his creation is preserved. God cannot cancel the consequences of rebellion without destroying morality, negating man's freedom, falsifying the very nature and structure of creation, and depriving man's knowledge of the utter seriousness of the Divine-human creative venture which is existence. The Covenant in all its seriousness must be preserved. This is life: God and man joined by Divine Will in copartnership, but never in such a way that either Divine Initiative or human responsibility is undercut. In a morally and meaningfully structured universe the consequences of inauthentic existence must be paid in full, or evil will lose all meaning, and meaning will become meaningless. An easy forgiveness makes for spoiled and indifferent rebels. At the very core of *the* revelation must be the overwhelming, living awareness of the terrifying burden and yet exhilarating majesty of the Divine Gift of and Call to freedom.

THE SECOND ADAM

And so, out of love, God forgives. But because it is forgiveness given not for its own sake but from and for love, it is done in such a way that the seriousness of sin and its consequences are part of the knowledge gained through forgiveness. Jesus undergoes the ruthless consequences of sin, enduring all that man in his selfishness can do to another, even unto a cross, and still God forgives. The literal consequences of sin are evil, suffering, despair, and death; these God does not remove, for this would be to undercut human freedom by denying to man the results of his freedom. Rather, on the one hand, God insists upon the full consequences of sin, and, on the other, for those who are willing to accept this Divine Act in their behalf, undergoes himself these full consequences. In effect, what

Adam was asked to do in regard to creation is now what every man is asked to do in regard to the Incarnation, the fullest possible revelation of God's nature and purpose. The overwhelming offer of copartnership to man, however, now involves far more. Not only is man recalled to the completion of creation, but man must be restored in order for this cosmic task to be undertaken.

ATONEMENT

The spirit necessary for understanding the Christian's insistence upon atonement is found in a story from the law courts. The son of a famous judge was apprehended for a crime, and brought into court to face judgment at the hands of his father. The judge heard all; but, at the conclusion of the trial, he imposed upon his son the stiffest fine which the law permitted. Then the judge rose to his feet, removed his robes, and, with his arm around his son's shoulders, paid the fine.

There is a real tension between justice and forgiveness, righteousness and accepting love. In the case of the judge, however, the tension was overcome. The integrity of law, order, and morality was preserved through justice, and the love of a father was given full expression. And what is more, it was not simply a matter of qualities being expressed without conflict, but

forgiving love was an instrument for the restoration of
the son to moral order, for the seriousness of his mis-
deed was engraved indelibly on the memory of the
boy.

These are part of the truths gleaned from common-
day living to which the Christian points in trying to
understand the meaning of Christ's act unto death. The
result has been that view of the atonement which is
called "objective" or "moral." The moral God cannot
overlook immorality without destroying his own nature. What is involved in human immorality is not simply human mistakes or carelessness. Man's immoral acts
are really acts of treason, for he who is a creature of
God opens up creation to the enemy by abandoning his
"sentry post" and fleeing. All meaning would be lost,
all human activity, even rebellion, made of no consequence, unless the consequences of such treason were
paid in full. To overlook man's wrongdoing would be
to upset the moral order of the universe and make God
an accomplice in evil. Man has dishonored God to the
best of his ability, has destroyed creation as best he
can, and there can be no escaping the punishment if
man is to be man and God is to be God.

And yet in receiving the justice of his own ways,
man has placed himself in a position from which he
cannot escape. How can man, who already owes perfect obedience to God, restore by his activity the God-
man relation? There is no answer except one: That

God's love for man is so inconceivably great that God himself will become man. If man is redeemed by Jesus Christ, the Christian holds, it can only be because God was incarnate in Christ.

That is to say, God does not owe reparation to himself; it is man who stands guilty before God. Consequently, he who redeems must be a man who in his perfect obedience owes no debt of his own, and as perfect can give more than is required: unmerited suffering voluntarily accepted in behalf of his fellow men. Yet he must also be God: in some sense, covered by the word "incarnation," such vicarious suffering must also be the suffering of God himself. God judges, and it is this God who undergoes the judgment. Jesus Christ must be "fully God and fully man." Only in this way can both the order of creation be preserved and man restored for his task in God's plan for creation. In Christ, a new relation is brought into being, the relation of man to God the Redeemer, that man may be restored to his relation in existence with God the Creator. In Jesus Christ the unity of God is preserved; in Jesus Christ God's willed copartnership with man is made an historical fact.

There are two other traditional views of the atonement that likewise help to expose other indispensable ingredients of this central Divine-human act. The "classical," "ransom," or "dramatic" understanding sees reconciliation occurring in the very act of Incarnation. God and evil are in dramatic conflict, waging battle for the souls of men. In Jesus Christ, the power of God is incarnated into finite man in his bondage and helplessness so that man emerges as a new creature.

The Incarnation marks a new beginning, for Jesus Christ is the completion, the fulfillment of the Divine Work begun in creation. In Christ the Divine Plan for creation is known in foretaste and beginning by those who accept the vision and the new Divine-human relation established by the Incarnation. This understanding is important, for the Incarnation reveals God himself as in real conflict with the powers of evil, for he himself, by his own choice, is powerless to destroy evil. In choosing freedom for man, the overcoming of the evil emerging from human rebellion cannot be God's doing alone, for this would be the destruction and bankruptcy of creation. Only God through man in his freedom can restore and complete creation in the intense struggle against the possibilities and actualities of evil. In Jesus Christ, Divine Intent and human response, Divine Power and human freedom, are perfectly united without destruction of any element.

As a result, this Divine-human act is the center of history, for it is in man's response to this one fulfillment of creation that the destiny of God's creative venture is to be determined. We shall have opportunity to return to this fundamental point again as we consider how such a thing as the Incarnation can occur.

The third understanding of atonement is traditionally called "subjective." Here the problem that is recognized is the need to transform the heart of man. Since sin centers in the human will, so it is the human will that must be transformed. To this end, the act of Jesus Christ is clearly intended.

In the first place, Jesus Christ so displays the infinite love of God that man's total attitude toward God is changed, for the positive dimension of the enigma of creation is revealed. He who is Creator of the world is revealed as He who suffers with and for his creation. Second, through Jesus Christ man sees himself pictured in all his rebelliousness, for it is human sin in its most revealing form that crucifies Him who comes in love to save. And third, in such a shattering of pride, a new self emerges, so characterized by love that one can understand the change only as the abiding presence of Christ himself.

INCARNATION AND THE HUMAN DILEMMA

Although these traditional views are usually offered as alternative understandings, it can be seen that each touches on some crucial aspect of the total Divine Act. Their fuller meaning, however, taken as a whole, can be understood only by perceiving how the Incarnation answers the human dilemma in which each of us now stands.

As we have indicated, the roots of the indifferent or demonic creation rest in man's disruption of the created order, his elevation of self to the status of Deity. By so doing, man forfeits his Divine-human destiny of creativity. Even an awareness of the error of his rebellion is not sufficient for establishing the vitality of authentic, fulfilled existence.

The dilemma is that the selfish will cannot selfishly will to make itself selfless. It is this impotence of egocentricity that is the core of the human problem. Through the biblical revelation, culminating in Jesus Christ, the ideal of human life which brings the fulfillment for which man is Divinely structured is made known. The ideal is God, self, and neighbor in a constant community of reciprocal love.

One can begin to participate in the meaning of the Garden of Eden by seeing it as the emergence of every child into the world. From the moment that the child is born, the self is the center of his life. He is hungry, and he cries; he is wet, and he screams. He expects the world to jump in response to his every whim and fancy, even at three o'clock in the morning. This is not to make the child into a villain, but simply to point out that this is the way that he is, and this is not the community of love.

The real dilemma, however, arises from the fact that we never really change. The meaning of the fall can be seen time after time as the child leaves the state of naïve innocence in the "moment" of self-consciousness. In coming to the state of responsibility, self-centeredness simply becomes more subtle. We never lose the priority of the self. Why? Because man's overarching need is to be accepted—to be loved. As the Christian insists—and contemporary psychology and psychiatry document—without love, without acceptance, man becomes only a dwarfed stump of his potential nature. When a person comes to self-consciousness, he continues the pattern present from birth—to become acceptable by striving to be accepted. This is *eros* love.

Whom do we love—the pimply-faced person down the street who desperately needs a friend, or those in whose company we feel important, the president of the right club, those whose likes conform to our own, those who fill our needs? In fact, do we seek friends at all because we desire to help others, or simply because we desire to have friends? And if we love God at all, is it not for the sake of receiving something from him, whether it be peace of mind or more noticeable success?

The self always gets in the way of real love relations, *agape* relations. This is because our driving motive, whether conscious or unconscious, is to get others to love us. We build up a façade so that others will accept us for what we wish them to think we are. The human strategy is to be accepted by enough of the "right" people so that we can accept ourselves as being what they think we are. To live, we must justify our lives, feel wanted, believe that we have a rightful place in life. We cannot live otherwise, and yet what this means is that all our activities find their essential motive in ourselves, in *our* wants, *our* values.

Authentic existence centers at the point of motive, not external consequence. The fulfilled man, the man living as he was created to be, is one whose actions are motivated by *agape*. Whatever a person does, if he himself is self-centered, the community of love is being perverted. This is why Luther made what seems at first glance to be an absurd statement: "All our righteousness is as filthy rags." What he meant was that all human acts are misdirected and thus perverse if their motive is the satisfaction and aggrandizement of the self. The morality of an act depends on *why* one does what he does. The coward who in his fleeing the battle accidentally misleads the enemy and saves the patrol can hardly be lauded for his courage.

Not only does man's pride undermine God's cosmic purpose, but, looked at only from the human perspective, it is self-defeating. To be loved, one must be lovable; yet the more one tries to be accepted, the more selfish he becomes, and, consequently, the more unlovable he really is. Nor can real acceptance and security be obtained in this way, for such acceptance depends on satisfying the fluctuating whims of others. At best, *eros* is an unstable and frustrating relation.

Religiously conceived, the attempt to love God can only be erotic, the attempt to receive; even the attempt to earn salvation or acceptance by God is self-defeating.

For the Christian, it is in Christ that the answer to this dilemma is found. In Christ is revealed the Incarnate Love of God supremely extended toward man. Epitomized in the cross, the believer sees God accepting him *despite his unacceptability*. Man kills the very Incarnation of God's love, and yet from the very threshold of death God loves and forgives.

This is complete *agape*, this is God's special act which establishes for one who believes a new relationship. Now one can love, not to gain anything from God or others, but because he has *already* received everything—total acceptance, total love, total forgiveness. As John says, we love because He *first* loved us. Through God's love, the basic need of man is met— one *is* accepted by the only Power worth being accepted by. Augustine expresses it thus: "You need no longer seek the way; behold, the way has come to you —pick up your bed and walk."

The unbeliever can enter the scriptural portrait of "the lamb of God," feel from within how all things are made new, if in the face of this tortured creature one is indeed encountering the forgiving love of God. No one can escape the power of this act, but to be so grasped that one cries out, "My Lord and my God," for this, one can only pray. The love of God in Christ must be more than an intellectual affair; one must experience this love as true for one's self.

Yet even the unbeliever can understand what such living faith in Christ could do to a man. To the degree that one believes in Christ as God's special act of accepting love, to that degree is the self purified of its self-centeredness. Now the motive for a man's activities becomes gratitude. One still loves God the Giver in an *eros* way, but it is transformed into *nonpossessive eros*. That is, God is loved not in order to force him to do anything; he is loved because of what he *has already done*.

One's relationships with others can be purified, for the possibility of loving others with *agape* is opened. No longer need I place myself between myself and the neighbor. My concern is not with what the neighbor can do for me, for I am already accepted; I have no need of the acceptance by others in order to accept myself. I can be concerned with the neighbor for his sake, because his needs are now mine. Through the Holy Spirit, God's love as an abiding presence, this realization of *agape* is a process that permits infinite creative development.

The Problem of Freedom and Grace

It is at this point that difficulty often arises. If this new life is the result of one's decision, it is self-salvation; yet, if man's response is simply God through the Holy Spirit answering himself, how can it really be man who responds? Unfortunately, traditional theologians often make living faith sterile by forcing it into logical molds. So here, theologians insist on an "either-or," coming down either with a "Pelagianism" that turns the Incarnation into a human example, or a "predestinarianism" that, with such as Calvin, elects and damns individuals "from the foundation of the earth."

There is no question for the Christian that the selfish will cannot unwill its selfishness without God's act in Jesus Christ. It would seem clear, likewise, that the "predestinarian" view undermines the whole Christian world-view; if God creates man free and yet redeems some through irresistible grace, the unanswerable question immediately arises: "Why, then, did God not determine man in the first place, thereby making evil and suffering impossible?" If there is no Divine Risk, then the problem of evil is insoluble, and human meaning is reduced simply to divine monologue.

The clue to this crucial problem of freedom and grace is to be found in the paradox posed by Paul: ". . . work out your *own* salvation with fear and trembling;

for *God is at work in you,* both to will and to work for
his good pleasure" (Philippians 2:12-13, italics mine).
From the side of the unbeliever, God offers his love
in the Incarnation, dramatically posed for man's choice
—grace is offered for man to receive. And yet, from
the side of faith, once one knows from within the
transforming meaning of this love, in humility he can
only confess, "Now I see whereas before I was blind;
I could never have come to this had thou not first
chosen me and guided my way." Just as God condemned the friends of Job for legislating from human
terms how God must act toward men, so the doctrine
of "election" dare not be made a logical attempt to
bind God. Even Calvin said, "Despite the mysteries of
God's election, it must be our prayer that all will be
saved." Election must be a humble confession of one's
personal inadequacies, never a systematic eradication
of human freedom or a cosmic census of Divine Activity. It is not a logical explanation, but a confession
of faith.

THE NATURE OF THE REDEEMED LIFE

A question which still remains is this: what actions
are required of man in this new Divine-human relationship? Does the Christian have a code to follow,
such as the Ten Commandments or the Beatitudes? De-

spite some interpreters of Christianity, the answer must
be "no." It is against such legalism that Jesus fought
most vehemently.

How, then, does one know what he is to do? The
answer is that he does not! Only two things does he
know. First, that whatever he does, it must be motivated in *agape;* second, whatever he does, its purpose
must be the establishment and furthering of the community of love. In other words, one's intent must be
increasingly to complete the triad of God-self-neigh-
bor in both depth and scope. The neighbor must be
brought into the reciprocal love from and toward
God. To this end, one must become Christ to his
neighbor, as Christ has been neighbor to the self. My
love must witness to the love I have received from God
and am in the process of sharing.

There are no absolute standards of right and wrong.
God himself said, "Thou shalt not kill." Yet this is the
same God who commanded death to certain enemies of
Israel. Jesus said, "Resist not evil," yet this is the same
Jesus who with a whip drove the money changers
from the temple; this is the Lord of love who said,
"I bring not peace but the sword." How are such
seeming inconsistencies to be understood?

Augustine summarizes the Christian life well: "Love
God and do what you will." The Christian life is a
matter of deciding from within each situation what is
best in that situation in order to bring others into the

responsible love relationship. What is good in one situation may be quite wrong in another. For example, when one faces a bully, he must decide how love dictates his action for bringing that individual into the triad of love. In one case, it might mean turning the other cheek, radiating a sense of the love that understands and accepts—this is the best way for *this* person to be brought to himself and truly exposed to the community of love in the making. In another case, however, what might be called for is out-and-out physical conflict—cheek turning would only permit this person another notch in his already well-vaunted pride. Only in receiving what he has given will he be brought to the humbling awareness of himself as he truly is.

Christian life is most difficult, for at its heart is freedom for love and love for freedom. This is the portrait that we have of Jesus, a portrait sketched with actions that are utterly inconsistent when reduced to a systematic code, yet perfectly consistent when measured by the demands of concrete love. It is for this reason that Jesus taught in parable. He related stories of particular situations, asking what the good would be in that situation—not what is good in general, but good in concrete incident. Consequently, to the rich young ruler Jesus said, "You lack one thing; go, sell what you have and give to the poor." This was in no way a universal injunction; it was an indication of the good for *this* man who had permitted wealth to rival his love of God and neighbor. Whatever keeps a person from the total love triad is wrong for that person, but for another it may be a powerful instrument for love. All things in creation are good, but all may be corrupted through human freedom.

The Christian life, then, has only one law: to love God with all one's heart, mind, soul, and strength, and one's neighbor as one's self. This injunction to "love your neighbor as yourself," however, should be changed from its usual meaning. It could be wrongly interpreted that one should love his neighbor selfishly. Its meaning is also richer than the natural morality of self-transcendence. For the Christian, its meaning is this: *one should love as he has been loved*—namely, with *agape*. One must love as he has been loved in Christ.

In the complex social sphere of contemporary life, specific actions emerging from this love motive may seem to involve considerable compromise with the present power structures, yet the Christian standard remains unaltered. Man's restoration and completion of creation must rest in the Divine Motive structuring creation—action out of love for the sake of love.

This, then, is the meaning of the Christian insistence upon Incarnation: Jesus Christ, the God-man, is the completion of the intent of creation in the life of man. He is the full revelation of the Divine-human venture of creativity to which man is drawn by the enigma of creation, and it is He who restores man for this vocation.

Yet two crucial problems still remain. First, the Christian must admit the Incarnation to be "a stumbling block to Jews and folly to Gentiles"; it is the "absurdity," as Kierkegaard called it. Yet, from the human perspective, can the occurrence of the Incarnation be so understood that although its mystery or miraculous quality is not removed, belief in it is rendered more than blind affirmation of that which is irrational, impossible, and inconceivable? Without some such understanding, the event remains so veiled that its transforming significance for all creation is lost.

This is to raise the second fundamental question: in what precise sense does the Incarnation not only say "yes" to the individual in his interpersonal relations, but provide as well the transforming meaning for all creation, for man's relations with nature, and, equally important, for his vocation as creator in the realm of culture?

*   *   *

In this chapter, we have found ourselves at the very heart of the Christian world-view. The meaning of Christianity is felt first in its ability to illuminate the nature of man and his dilemma. For this end, the portrait of Adam stands without rival. Herein is every man, standing between the animals and God, as the free agent in God's cosmic plan.

In his freedom, man doubts, man rebels, he relies on himself, he regards himself as though he were God. But man is a creature, not God, and the proof of the lie of human supremacy is the living of it. Man is made for *agape*, selfless love, and when one makes all things a means for meeting his needs, frustration is inevitable. The more actively one pursues that which will quiet his anxiety, the further one drives himself from the meaning which fulfills.

It is within this experience of the human dilemma that the Old Testament writers understood history. Creation is for Covenant, for the Divine-human task of completing creation. But time after time in Israel's history, God's creative call was swallowed up in man's rebellious response.

Out of the frustration of human history appeared the mysterious person of Jesus Christ. In this man the Christian beholds more than a man, for through him man is shaken to honesty about himself, forgiveness is offered, evil finds an answer, and love in its infinite, Divine depths is exhibited. Those who have lived "in Christ" testify to a peace, a fullness, a completion that is self-justifying, that is its own witness that he who creates and he who redeems are one.

Edwin Markham put it well: "In Love is all the law we need, in Christ is all the God we know."

6

INCARNATION AND THE STRUCTURE OF CREATION

> For it is the God who said, "Let light shine out of darkness," who has shone in our hearts to give the light of the knowledge of the glory of God in the face of Christ.
>
> —II Corinthians 4:6

JESUS CHRIST WAS, IS, AND WILL always remain a figure of mystery. Even the disciples were unable to understand him clearly during his lifetime, often misinterpreting his meaning, and attempting at almost every crucial juncture to deter him from completing his ministry. In fact, with the climaxing event of the Crucifixion imminent, the disciples deserted, returning to their former vocations in the belief that their faith had ended in disaster. It was only from the perspective of the Resurrection that the meaning of the total Christ-event became understandable; through faith in this fact the disciples saw every event in Christ's life transformed.

Consequently, the account of Jesus that we have in

196]

the New Testament is not that written with the eye of an uninvolved reporter. It is clearly and unabashedly an interpretation, written some years after the events themselves by persons whose lives had been transfigured by the figure they portrayed. Not only were the events of Christ's life reinterpreted from the perspective of this faith, but what had happened to these disciples provided the overwhelming impetus for reinterpreting the Old Testament as well from this new perspective. Such phrases as these permeate the New Testament: "As it was written . . . ," "In order to fulfill Scripture . . . ," "It was told to you of old, but I say unto you . . . ." For the New Testament writers, all life takes its meaning from the center point of history—Jesus Christ. There is no other way for the Christian to understand God's work in history than as "Creation through Covenant for Incarnation."

"Who Do You Say That I Am?"

Yet who is this Jesus? Scripture supplies only meager information concerning his parentage and early life. In fact, Mark, the writer of the original Gospel, begins his story with Jesus at the age of thirty. Matthew and Luke, on the other hand, point to the uniqueness of Jesus through such a story as the Virgin Birth, a story which neither Mark nor Paul knew. Such stories function to underscore the unparalleled nature of

Jesus, but they are of little help in understanding him. We see the difficulty which these disciples encountered in comprehending the Incarnation when we remember that Matthew traces Jesus' ancestry in detail through Joseph to Abraham, and Luke through Joseph to Adam, trying to give real content to his humanity; yet both authors proceed to undermine all this by affirming that Joseph was not the father at all—Jesus was born of a virgin and the Holy Spirit.

It is apparent here that the Gospel writers began with one central fact, and from this beginning attempted to infer what they did not know for certain. This fact was that through Jesus Christ a transformed life had come to them, that, behold, this event had made all things new. And the urgent question followed: if salvation comes through Jesus Christ, "who, then, do you say that I am?" In a manner beautiful in its simplicity, Matthew and Luke could only answer in story form, this is Incarnation, He is both man and God, even though in so saying one becomes committed to seeming contradictions.

INCARNATION AS A CONFESSION

When in the fourth and fifth centuries, the Church Fathers attempted to clarify this affirmation by means of the Nicene (A.D. 325) and Chalcedonian (A.D. 451) Creeds, they found themselves beset by the selfsame difficulty. Athanasius reaffirmed the biblical method in clarifying the rationale for confessing the Trinity. The Trinitarian affirmation was no attempt to blueprint the Divine Nature but was a confession of faith. Redemption can come only from God, and since the Christian has known redemption through Jesus Christ, there is no escaping the conclusion: one must affirm that God himself was in Christ. If Christ were only a man, such redemption would come only from a human, and this would not be "saving." Yet if Christ is not at least man, how can the human be said to be redeemed by, in, and through him? It is man's fallen and rebellious nature that must be assumed if man is to be transformed, and yet it must be God himself who does the assuming. The Christian must affirm the doctrine of the Trinity, insisting therein upon Jesus Christ as the God-man, the Incarnation of God himself in human nature. Nothing less than such an affirmation can account for the transformation effected by Christ.

THE LIMITS OF THE CREED

The philosophical category of the day available for the Church Fathers to state this was the Greek term, *ousia*, meaning "nature." Jesus was one in *nature* with God, as well as one in *nature* with man. This was the statement chosen at Chalcedon to express it:

One and the same Christ, Son, Lord, Only-begotten, in two natures, inconfusedly, unchangeably, indivisibly, inseparably, the distinction of natures being by no means taken away by the union, but rather the property of each nature being preserved and concurring in one person and one subsistence, not parted or divided into two persons, but one and the same Son and Only-begotten, God the Word, the Lord Jesus Christ.

Such a confession is of some value in setting out channel markers that protect the central affirmation of Christianity; but rather than making the Christ-event more understandable, such a creed only intensifies the confusion. Through the years, it has been this Creed of Chalcedon concerning the Incarnation that has been one of the most unsatisfactory of all Christian formulations.

CHRIST AND CREATION

Affirmations concerning the nature of Christ, however, have not been limited to faith inferences from the fact of personal redemption. Since the Christian affirms that Christ is the fulfillment and completion of God's cosmic purposes, the nature of Christ must be expressed in such a way as to affirm that Creation was and is for Incarnation. This affirmation was expressed in Scripture far more beautifully than the attempts made in the early creedal formulae. This is the confession with which John begins his Gospel:

> In the beginning was the Word, and the Word was with
> God, and the Word was God. He was in the beginning
> with God; all things were made through him, and with-
> out him was not anything made that was made. . . . He
> was in the world, and the world was made through him,
> yet the world knew him not. (1:1-3, 10)

Whatever else "Word" means, its most obvious reference is to the Genesis affirmation that God created all
things with a word—"And God said, 'Let there be
light.' "

Paul, in his Epistle to the Colossians, insists in like
manner upon Christ as the completer, fulfiller, and
transformer of all creation.

> He is the image of the invisible God, the first-born of
> all creation; for in him all things were created, in
> heaven and on earth, visible and invisible. . . . All things
> were created through him and for him. He is before all
> things, and in him all things hold together. . . . For in
> him all the fullness of God was pleased to dwell, and
> through him to reconcile to himself all things, whether
> on earth or in heaven, making peace by the blood of
> his cross. (1:15-20)

It is here, in relating Christ and creation that we have
one of the most central and lofty affirmations of all
Christianity. Yet the Incarnation has been so shrouded
by sterile philosophical jargon that such a confession
remains one of the most untapped and undeveloped
aspects of Christianity, even though Creation for In-

carnation is the faith-supposition underlying all other Christian doctrines. What does it really mean to affirm that "in him all the fullness of God was pleased to dwell"? Such a question need not be an idle curiosity concerning divine things; rather, such a question must be raised if the fullness of the Christian faith is to become effective in the total life of man.

In affirming that through Christ, God created all things that were created, what is being affirmed is that the structure, the essence, the nature, the meaning of all created things find their clue and fulfillment in the Incarnation. Consequently, the structure of creation, on the one hand, provides the clue for understanding the Incarnation, and, on the other, is that which is fully revealed and completed in the Incarnation.

CONTEMPORARY LITERATURE ON THE STRUCTURE OF CREATION

It is in exploring this crucial point that the enigma of creation being uncovered in our times becomes of real importance. You will remember that the awareness to which the literary writers of our time are coming is that man's cosmic alienation is the basis for both his social and self alienation. Only in finding a satisfactory solution for man's alienation from creation, they have held, can the self be united with its own being and with other beings.

At the heart of these literary searches for answer are those proposed by Sartre, Kafka, and Camus. Sartre puts the problem clearly. If there is a Creator God, then man is created with a specific essence or nature which must be discovered and fulfilled if selfhood is to be attained. In a phrase, essence would precede existence. Yet, Sartre insists, because God does not exist, man has no such essence to be realized. Man's task, consequently, is to become "god," to assume the task of creating one's own essence. The authentic, fulfilled self is one who chooses his own essence and lives in complete consistency with this free choice. It is in this manner that essence and existence are made one—this is "redemption."

Camus, however, is far less certain about the cosmic issue. It would seem that the cosmic powers, personal or impersonal, torture and destroy the very life they ground. But here is the important point. Has man an essence? In essay and in novel, Camus takes the affirmative. Herein rests his fundamental affinity with Kafka. In Kafka's *The Trial*, the tragedy of "K's" "death like a dog" depends on whether or not "K" has lived like a dog. There is nothing tragic in the doglike death of a dog. For Kafka, only in searching with utter intensity for cosmic meaning does one's death become a silent protest which, to use his words, "will outlast him." In effect, this is the affirmation that man is such that ultimate meaninglessness is a travesty upon his essential being. Man by nature is such that existence in ignorance, uncertainty, despair, and death is an affront which is inherently self-contradictory. This is the basis for man's eternal search for meaning: although all else may undercut hope in any ultimate meaning, man's essential being defies any such certain conclusion.

Camus' understanding comes as strong underscoring of this basic insight. Suffering, evil, death—that is, the plague which is life—is a blasphemy against human integrity. *It should not be*, not because of what man thinks, but *because of what man is*, potentially, however, rather than actually. The only answer for Camus is one of self-consistency in the face of cosmic agnosticism. Man's integrity can be actualized only if man defies those powers which seek to destroy it. Even though man's fight against suffering and evil may be ultimately of no consequence, like the endless rolling of Sisyphus' stone, it has existential validity for in such corporate protest man attains an integrity which renders cosmic indifference a travesty. When Camus' main character, Doctor Rieux, says, "What interests me is being a man," we have a testimony to a human essence which is a miracle in the midst of existence as it is.

This, too, is the witness of MacLeish in *J. B.* J. B. says to Sarah, "God does not love, He *is*." Or in Camus' terms, cosmic power is not concerned, it is indifferent. "But," Sarah replies, "we do. That's the wonder." Wonder, perhaps it is, but certainly enigma, that man is capable of selfless love in an indifferent cosmos, of nurturing human warmth in the midst of cosmic coldness, of remaining loyal despite cosmic disloyalty. "Blow on these coals," MacLeish suggests, "and we'll see by and by." See what? This is the question which he leaves to the audience, as he leaves it unanswered for himself. But the direction of his thinking is akin to Unamuno's literary method—"By probing deeply the character of man belonging to a time and a place, one can discover what is universal and common to all men. . . ."

To the degree that these contemporary literary analyses are discovering that in man which is universal, to that degree is Sartre's atheistic certainty being challenged. Although the implications here have not yet been fully drawn, increasingly the problem of human essence is becoming *the* problem which haunts the contemporary author; it is the problem which keeps him from following the logic of his aloneness, his alienation, his relativity, and his uncertainty, to the certain conclusion of utter cosmic meaninglessness.

This literary wrestling with the problem of human essence is illustrated well by the title of one of Luigi Pirandello's plays—"Six Characters in Search of an Author." Whatever else this play may mean, the suggestion is clear that man's life is so molded, essentially drawn, as it were, that the playwright-character analogy seems somehow to apply. If it be true that man is

not unlimited, but bounded, not simply as with Sartre
by a common situation confronting man, but by an
innate, interior structure, form, essential vitality, then
the search for man's essential nature is at the same time
the search for the meaning of creation. The Divine and
the human are indissolubly related by the very structure of man's created nature. Sartre is right; the affirmation of theism is an affirmation of human essence,
of the *imago Dei*. But the reverse is no less true: the
discovery of human essence is an affirmation of an
essential God-man relation. That is, God is implied by
the very fact of human nature, and his nature is revealed by the perfect fulfillment of human nature.

This dawning awareness accounts in large part for
the contemporary interest in the novels of Dostoevsky,
the greatest Christian novelist. Two questions obsess
Dostoevsky. The first is identical with the protests of
many of these contemporary literary writers: can man
live with God? That is, can the conditions of suffering
and evil possibly permit belief in a God? His positive
answer here we have already suggested. But Dostoevsky's second question is even more basic: can man live
without God? This, in effect, is to raise the question of
human essence. Is man so formed that either God must
exist or man must create Him in order to be a self?
This is what Unamuno means by the passion of life—
man's task is to so live as "to create truth because it
must be so."

Dostoevsky's novels trace the interior logic of man's existence, to conclude partly in *Crime and Punishment* and definitively in *The Brothers Karamazov* that a human essence is present for which the only options are the man-God, advocated by a Sartre, which is self-destructive, or the God-man, Jesus Christ, which brings discovery and fulfillment of the self. Dostoevsky's second question is the key question which is emerging in contemporary literature, but is often more felt than clearly realized.

The Christian Understanding of "Essence"

Such contemporary literary explorations as these witness to a Christian understanding of the structure of man that illuminates and in turn is illuminated by the Incarnation. Whether Roman Catholic or Protestant, the Christian affirms an essential analogy between man and God, that pointed to by the *imago Dei*.

For the Roman Catholic or Thomist, man is a composite of form and potency, driven by an impulse for actuality. Although man has freedom, this freedom cannot change the fact of this God-given form or nature. This can be illustrated. The essential form of an acorn is oak-treeness, and even the gift of freedom if given to an acorn could not provide it with the possibility of becoming a maple. Freedom means the capacity to fulfill essence or to deny it, but *not to lose it*.

In the fall, man rejects this essence by attempting to become what he is not. By trying to become more than a man, he becomes less than a man. This alienation from creation, from God, means inevitably an alienation of his existence from his essential nature.

With this understanding, the classical Protestant agrees. Life is the creative dialogue between one's existence and his essence. But in rejecting God, one's essence becomes an "ought" which man cannot attain; he experiences it as a craving, as an unidentified need which cannot be shaken. Of this condition, as we have said, Augustine speaks perceptively: "Lord, Thou hast made us for Thyself, and we are restless until we find our rest in Thee." That is, despite man's doings, he cannot remove from himself his essential nature, his "oughtness," which is love-fulfillment in God. In rebellion, one becomes a split creature, yearning for his real self. In reality, he is crying out for his Alpha and Omega.

Kierkegaard expresses this central Protestant analysis powerfully in his own subtle, satirical manner: "To strive to become what one already is; who would take the pains to waste his time on such a trifle?" Self-fulfillment is to truly be what through one's created structure he has about him to become. In *Sickness unto Death*, Kierkegaard brilliantly analyzes sin as having its basis in man's refusal to accept his essence, his refusal to become what his self is. For the Protestant, this essential self cannot be clearly identified nor fulfilled without the revelation of the perfect man. Jesus Christ is the fulfillment of the *imago Dei* and, as the perfect fulfillment of man's created nature, he is the supreme revelation of the nature of the Creator.

From the perspective of this revelation of Deity through perfect humanity, the enigma of creation is disclosed as an expression of the grace of creation— God working through the very structure of creation to expose the lie on the basis of which man is living. God will not permit man ever to rest content with inauthentic existence, with a hollow, divided, and un-creative self. Simone Weil speaks perceptively of "the infinitely tender love which has extended to me the gift of unhappiness." It is this negative grace that drives man to see in Jesus Christ the fulfillment of the creative tension between essence and existence.

THE INCARNATION AS PERFECT MANHOOD

In approaching the Incarnation from this perspective of the human dilemma, we can begin to understand what it means to say that in the man Jesus "the fullness of God was pleased to dwell." As perfect man, Jesus Christ is the fullness of the *imago Dei*, the image of himself in which God created man. In like manner we can begin to see the meaning of the affirmation that "all things were created through him and for him."

Through him is revealed a Divine Depth, an Essence, a Potentiality in all finite reality, in relation to which the Divine Gift of freedom comes as the Call to creativity, for which the goal is "the new heaven and the new earth." The understanding at which we have arrived is only one part of the meaning of the Incarnation, but it is an important part: in perfect humanity is the revelation of Divinity; and in the fulfillment of the potentialities of creation is exposed the glory, the nature, of God's cosmic enterprise. To a fuller understanding of this affirmation we shall turn later.

Jesus as "Truly Man"

The Christian also maintains that although Jesus Christ is the supreme revelation of the nature of Deity, God must be known in his fullness not only as Creator but also as Redeemer. To put this in another way, it is God's *Will* that must also be revealed. Despite the Divine-human destiny of creativity to which man is being called by creation, it is the dilemma of man that he is in rebellion against this Creator. Man stands guilty of defying this creative calling. To know God's nature is to know one's self as impotent, or in traditional terminology, to know one's self as sinner. How, then, are we to understand the Incarnation of God in the man Jesus so as to affirm that "God was *in* Christ, *reconciling* the world to himself"? This is another way of asking the perennial question, "How is it possible to affirm that the action of Jesus Christ was the very action of God himself—that 'I and the Father are one'?"

As we search gropingly for meaning here, it is abundantly clear from Scripture that Jesus was not God in the sense that he was a Deity who only looked like a man—Jesus was truly human. Christians have been prone to overlook this fact, for they seem embarrassed by it. But it is clear that no one can come to terms with the scriptural portrait who tries to pretend Jesus' humanity away. Was Jesus' knowledge infinite? —"But of that day or that hour no one knows, not even the angels in heaven, nor the Son, but only the Father" (Mark 13:32). Was Jesus absolutely perfect?—"Why do you call me good? No one is good but God alone" (Luke 18:19). Did Jesus know human temptation?— Satan said, "If you, then, will worship me, it shall all be yours" (Luke 4:7). Did Jesus know human agony? —"And being in an agony, he prayed more earnestly; and his sweat became like great drops of blood falling down upon the ground" (Luke 22:44). Did Jesus know human despair?—"My God, my God, why hast thou forsaken me?" (Matthew 27:46). Did Jesus have human freedom?—". . . not my will, but thine, be done" (Luke 22:42).

COVENANT AS THE NATURE OF FULFILLED EXISTENCE

To understand how Jesus in all his humanity can be
understood as being at the same time the Incarnation
of God himself, we must return to the idea of Covenant in which Jesus understood himself as standing.
The Covenant was God's pledge of loyalty to Israel,
demanding obedience to God's Will in every moment
of Israel's existence. The content of God's Will, according to the prophetic tradition, was not something
dictated once and for all. It was not composed of rules
and rituals to be followed for their own sake. What
the Covenant relation demanded in each moment was
revealed *in that moment*—the Covenant goal was to be
increasingly revealed and discovered through the ongoing Divine-human dialogue which is history.

It is for this reason that the Scripture appears as a
record of God's calling of individuals within a living
tradition, individuals who were created and nurtured
for the revelation and accomplishment of God's concrete Will for men. Adam, Noah, Abraham, Moses,
Gideon, Amos, Hosea, Isaiah, Jeremiah, John the Baptist, Jesus, the Disciples, Paul—Scripture records the
special call of each of these, and together they and
others like them compose the fabric of God's activity.

To see this fact is to perceive that man is composed
of more than a universal or *general* nature held in common. God creates not in general but in particular; each

individual is sacred, singular, unprecedented. Each self is created as he is because God would have it so. Each individual, then, has a *concrete* nature which is his and his alone. One way of pointing to this concrete or special nature as over against one's general nature is to say that although all men have the same potentialities, each individual has these capacities to a different degree and together they compose a different pattern.

It is the Covenant witness that the Will of God is discovered as each unique individual encounters each new historical situation as a fresh moment of creation. It is through this creative dialogue that the special Divine-human calling emerges for each person in his freedom to accept or reject. At the heart of the Christian understanding is this affirmation of the sanctity of human life; each is precious in the sight of God, for in each is a creative potentiality which will either be realized in that special life situation, or of it the world will be eternally deprived. God's Will is abiding and all-encompassing, but it is personal and immediate, extending, as Jesus insisted, to sparrows of the air, the lilies of the field, indeed, can we believe it, to each hair of one's head.

It is in Jesus that we see this personal life under Covenant brought to perfection. It is a life lived without any other regard than the Will of God in each moment:

If God so clothes the grass of the field, which today is alive, and tomorrow is thrown into the oven, will he not much more clothe you, O men of little faith? Therefore do not be anxious, saying, 'What shall we eat?' or 'What shall we drink?' or 'What shall we wear?' . . . Your heavenly Father knows that you need them all. (Matthew 6:30-32)

This is utter faith in the personal and immediate providence of God to provide and to lead in every moment —this is the Covenant relation incarnated in its fullness.

COVENANT AS A CLUE TO THE INCARNATION

This lived Covenant faith provides not only a revelation of the pattern of God's Will for every man, but it provides a clue for understanding the Incarnation as *the* revelation of the Divine Will. The writer of the Gospel of Mark was greatly concerned about the fact that Jesus did not early and consistently declare himself to be the Christ, the Messiah. To account for this peculiarity, Mark developed the idea of the "Messianic secret." That is, although Jesus never denied that he was the Messiah, he told his disciples, for reasons not always clear, that they should not tell others who he was.

Simple though this explanation is, it only raises more forcefully the question of how Jesus understood himself. Since this was a real problem for the biblical writers themselves, there can be no clear answer, but the question cannot be avoided. Little is known of Jesus' early life, yet the stories which we do have suggest strongly that the boy Jesus did not fully understand himself as the Messiah. He "must be about his Father's business," but that he knew exactly what that really involved for him is in real doubt. The portrait that we have suggests rather one of growth, of a developing consciousness of himself as set aside for a very special task designated by God. He "increased in wisdom and in stature, and in favor with God and man" (Luke 2:52).

The nature of the Jewish Messianic faith and the crisis situation of Israel in Jesus' time were such as to make inevitable to such a devout and gifted youth as he the constant question as to whether or not *he* was the Messiah, the Chosen One, or if "there is to be another." Messiahship comes only from God. One cannot be Messiah by virtue of his own right; only by being Divinely chosen is such a destiny possible. The man Jesus could never explicitly declare himself to be the Messiah, at least not at the beginning, for it was not his decision to make. Jesus, standing fully within the Covenant tradition, saw as his sole task that of maintaining complete "oneness" with God in each moment, striving through prayer and the Spirit which he felt within himself to do whatever the Will of God might dictate in each action for each unique situation. If the path through which he was thus led was that of Messiahship, so be it; if not, he had served his God in the role which God had willed. He could do no more, and would do no less.

Jesus' life in Nazareth is obscure. It was the appearance of a new prophet who seemed in every way to fulfill the Old Testament prophecies concerning the forerunner of the Messiah that seemed to challenge Jesus to put to the test the meditations of his heart. Upon his inchoate Messianic consciousness, contact with John the Baptist had decisive effect. He saw, in the multitudes surrounding the Baptist, proof that a great movement of repentance and expectation had set in. He heard the prophetic pronouncement of the imminent appearance of the Messiah, and went forth from his own baptism to the wilderness wherein to search out the nature of the part which he now was convinced he was being called to play. He, as Israel before him, was led into the desert to be disciplined into knowledge of his part within the Covenant meaning.

The Gospels leave no question that Jesus knew the ancient Scriptures thoroughly. It was no doubt largely through these that Jesus sought, while in the wilderness and later, for a fuller understanding of his Divine calling. One is led by Jesus' teachings and the total impression of his life to conclude that it was in Isaiah's prophecy concerning the "suffering servant" that he came increasingly to find illumination concerning his own unique nature and calling. According to Mark, a time came early in his ministry when Jesus withdrew from the publicity which his call to repentance had stimulated, wandering with his disciples to the North. It was then that he began to speak to his followers first of the relation which he understood existing between Messiahship and suffering. Yet not even then did he declare himself to be the Chosen One.

It is in the temptation accounts after his baptism that we see portrayed best Jesus' attitude toward himself. As "fully man," Jesus felt the urge to proclaim himself, to affirm his uniquely felt relationship with God and his growing belief in his special calling. Yet he knew that to test this call by throwing himself down from the Temple pinnacle, to see if God would save him as he would if he were the Messiah, was to tempt God, to attempt to force God's hand. He knew that to so act would be to deny his Messiahship, if indeed he possessed it. It should be noted that each of his temptations were temptations to either affirm or deny by action the role of Messiahship.

In his reply to John the Baptist, we see perhaps the most striking example of this understanding of Jesus. John's followers put the question to him directly: "Are you he who is to come, or shall we look for another?" (Luke 7:19). Jesus could not dogmatically reply in the affirmative, for the Father alone can know this with certainty. Notice especially his reply: "Go and tell John what you have seen and heard." The meaning to be drawn from his accompanying words would seem to be this: "I can tell you no more than what you have seen and heard. Do not the blind receive their sight and the lame walk; are not the lepers cleansed, the deaf healed, the dead raised, and the good news preached to the poor? Is this not what was prophesied concerning the Messiah? Could this be done if it were not God working through his Chosen One? To you, the God-chosen forerunner of the Messiah, I ask: does it not seem to be I of whom you have born witness?" Jesus' response was not in the indicative, but in the interrogative. The answer was one that Jesus himself was struggling to know.

On another occasion, Jesus put the matter this way: "If I am not doing the works of my Father, then do not believe me." And still again, we find this episode in John's Gospel: "So the Jews gathered round him and said to him, 'How long will you keep us in suspense? If you are the Christ, tell us plainly.' Jesus answered them, . . . 'The works that I do in my Father's name, they bear witness to me.'" (10:24-25). Throughout, the question which he asked of others was heavy on his own mind—"Who do you say that I am?"

PROPHECIES CONCERNING THE MESSIAH

Modern Christians have difficulty understanding the correlation between Old Testament "prophecies" and the words and actions of Jesus as recorded in the New Testament. This amazing correlation has led many scholars to hold that many things recorded in the Gospels are additions made by the early Church in order to witness more powerfully to its claim that Jesus was the Messiah.

Easy as this explanation is on the sensitivity of our scientific minds, it is an explanation of mixed value. Since such correlations are so frequent, so closely related to the central affirmations of Christianity, and so important for the Gospel writers themselves, such undercutting at this point brings into serious question the veracity of the New Testament throughout. If our reconstruction based on Scripture is accurate, however, these correlations can be understood as being, to a great degree, historical fact. It was through a constant dialogue between the Will of God revealed in prayerful encounter with each situation and the Will of God speaking through Scripture that Jesus attempted to be led in each moment. Especially as Jesus "turned his head steadfastly toward Jerusalem" in the latter days of his life does it seem that the Will of God for him was revealed in the writings of the Old Testament prophets.

The activities of Jesus had led not to "glorious Messiahship," but, from a purely human perspective, to failure. Ironically, however, this increasing "failure" led Jesus not to disillusionment concerning his emerging Messianic self-consciousness, but to see in such "failure" the portrait of the "suffering servant" emerging as fact and as call. Through such illumination he no longer regarded his rejection by the Jews as a living denial of his Messiahship, but as a revelation of Israel's sin, of its perversion of God's promises, of its final rejection of the Covenant. The pattern of the Old Testament continued in the present and disclosed the pattern of God's Will now for Jesus. In this living context of common-day life, Jesus came to see in Isaiah's "suffering servant" God's intent for him—in death he would "bear the sins of many," ransoming them from both their "spiritual" leaders and themselves. In so doing, men would be readied for the Kingdom whose coming was in God's hands. Death was the goal set by God for him. So understanding the fullness of his task as the Servant, he went with assurance to his death, witnessing by bold action the truth about himself—"I am the Christ."

The correlation between the Old Testament and the life of Jesus can thus be largely understood not as insertions made after the fact but as facts brought into being by him who saw in Scripture the concrete Will of the Father for his life.

Jesus as "Truly God"

One of the most revealing illustrations of this attitude of Jesus toward his unique vocation appears in the last days of his life. "Father, if thou art willing, remove this cup from me; nevertheless not my will, but thine, be done" (Luke 22:42). Throughout the Gospels, oneness of the man Jesus with the Father is presented as a oneness of Wills. In the Gospel of John, for example, we find these statements: "My food is to do the will of him who sent me, and to accomplish his work" (4:34); "I can do nothing on my own authority; . . . I seek not my own will but the will of him who sent me" (5:30); ". . . this is the will of him who sent me, that I should lose nothing of all that he has given me . . ." (6:39).

The manifestation of this oneness of Will was in concrete activity: "If I am not doing the works of my Father, then do not believe me; but if I do them, even though you do not believe me, believe the works, that you may know and understand that the Father is in me and I am in the Father" (John 10:37-38). In like manner, it is affirmed that in doing the Will of Jesus, men "may all be one; even as thou, Father, art in me, and I in thee" (John 17:21).

Before developing further this understanding of the Incarnation in terms of "Will," the reader must understand clearly that we are insisting completely upon the orthodox claim that Jesus Christ is the God-man. We wish to declare uncompromisingly what the Christian must affirm, that the Christ event is the activity of *God*. It will not do to see here only the ascending career of a man who was successful in the sphere of religion. For the Christian to see only this is to threaten Christianity at its heart.

Yet the difficulty with the orthodox formulations is that they insist upon two natures in Jesus, a Divine nature and a human nature. Such an insistence as this, however, has no meaning at all unless we speak also of two consciousnesses. But, according to the creed, these two natures are in one personality. Beyond such a meaningless, inconceivable posing of the Incarnation, orthodox theologians have been unable to go.

We have developed a far more promising basis for understanding the Incarnation in our distinguishing in every man between essence and existence. As we have indicated, there is a general essence universal to man as such. There is also in every human a concrete essence, that is, a concrete potentiality of this common essence, which is the God-given possibility unique for that man. The division between essence and existence is not an expression of fallenness. It is the God-created distinction contained in the gift of freedom through which man under God comes to creativity.

In a real sense, everything in creation becomes the incarnation of the nature of the Creator God to the degree that it comes to this creative fullness. Yet the

Will of God for each thing differs, for the Divinely created potential in each is unique. Paul put it this way: "Having gifts that differ according to the grace given to us, let us use them: if prophecy, in proportion to our faith, if service, in our serving; . . . he who contributes, in liberality; he who gives aid, with zeal; he who does acts of mercy, with cheerfulness" (Romans 12:6-8).

This being true, we have our clue for understanding the Incarnation: *only for one Man was his unique essence that of Divine Sonship.* Though it was God's Will to manifest himself in particular ways in Moses, in Abraham, and in Isaiah, only for Jesus was it God's Will that his words and deeds, in fact his very being, be the very acts of forgiveness, of acceptance, of love, the very Incarnation, of God himself. In the oneness of the human will of this man with the total and complete concrete Will of God for him, we have an act of full Divinity in which the Covenant becomes a physical reality. What Jesus did, God himself has done, for God has willed that it be in this man that his total Will for man may be both revealed and Incarnated in complete realization.

The New Testament leaves no doubt that Jesus was free, with a will of his own that knew temptation. He was free to reject his unique calling, but in his freedom he "did not count equality with God a thing to be grasped, but *emptied himself*, taking the form of a

servant. . . he humbled himself and *became obedient*
unto death, even death on a cross" (Philippians 2:6-8).
This is the miracle of the Incarnation, that God willed
to make his total Will one with this man, that God
willed in the washing of feet to enter humbly into
Divine-human partnership, that in his death God too
underwent suffering, in his words of forgiveness God
himself forgives, and through his Resurrection God
himself is transforming the whole created order. This
is the miracle, that in the destiny set for Jesus, those
who perceive in faith can believe that "ye who have
seen me have seen the Father." "I glorified Thee on
earth, having accomplished the work which thou
gavest me to do" (John 17:4).

*   *   *

In this chapter, we have come to some understanding
of how the Incarnation can be. The traditional affirmation of the creed that Jesus Christ is fully God and
fully man expresses the implications of redemption
that the Christian has known through him, and yet
there remains the urgent question of what such an
affirmation as this could possibly mean.

Instead of seeking understanding in terms of two
"natures," as is usually done, we found a more promising basis in the distinction between "essence" and
"existence" testified to in contemporary thought. All

that God creates is incomplete, but rather than being a deficiency, such incompleteness is the foundation for the call to man for copartnership in bringing the existence of things into harmony with their potentialities, their essential natures. To the degree that anything gains the fullness of its Divinely intended structure, it is a "revelation" of the Creator himself.

Likewise, in the perfect humanity of Jesus Christ we have the perfect, the most complete revelation of Deity, for the essence completed in Jesus Christ is the *imago Dei* in man, the image of God himself. And not only is the nature of God perfectly revealed, but Christ is the revealer, the pattern, the measure of all else in existence. Through him a Divine depth is known to reside in everything, and this potential fullness of being comes as "call" to man to accept the Divine-human destiny of creativity. Creation is ongoing; it is demand, invitation, call.

Not only is the nature of God and the nature of his creation revealed through Jesus Christ, but through him man is restored to copartnership with God for the cosmic task. For man's rebellion to be negated, forgiven, and man restored to the freedom of Eden, a special act by God is required. It is here that perhaps the most difficult question of all is to be found: how can it be that "God was *in* Christ, reconciling the world to himself"?

At this point we found our clue in the Covenant.

Although each man has a general nature held in common with other men, each individual is unique in terms of the particular pattern which these potentialities form in him. God's activity in history centers in the calling of individuals for specific tasks. The fulfillment of each self and the fulfillment of God's Covenant-Will for history consists in one's free acceptance of God's concrete Will as one's own.

On the basis of this understanding, we considered the New Testament portrait of Jesus, finding much to support an understanding of Jesus in these terms. The overarching intent of Jesus was to so subordinate his will to the Will of the Father that in every moment he would be led to act, think, and be as God had destined him.

As God's intent for each man differs, as each man's concrete essence is special to the Divine Plan, so in Jesus. Of him alone, the Christian confesses, was his unique essence that of Divine Sonship. In his free acceptance of God's Will, in his perfect obedience of the Father, the Divine Will to redeem man was fully realized: in the humbling, suffering, forgiving love of this Man is the very humbling, suffering, forgiving love of God himself. "In him all the fullness of God was pleased to dwell . . . ," for God has willed it so.

It is from this understanding of the structure of creation that we began to understand how the Incarnation can be. It is from this understanding of the Incarnation, in turn, that the fuller meaning of creation is revealed. It is to the fuller implications of the Incarnation for the transformation of creation that we now turn.

INCARNATION AND THE TRANSFORMATION OF CREATION

7

There is a beauty at the goal of life,
A beauty growing since the world began . . .
    —Archibald Lampman, "The Largest Life" [1]

THERE ARE TWO FUNDAMENTAL intellectual tasks for the Christian. The first is to understand in depth the central events at the heart of his faith. The second is to look from the perspective of this understanding upon all creation in order to expose the transforming meaning of these events for all things. It is in the biblical account of the revelation in Jesus Christ that the Christian gains the basis of his faith. But since this event is the key to the essential meaning of all things, Scripture cannot be regarded as the end of man's religious understanding. Just as the biblical writers reinterpreted the Old Testament from the perspective of the Christ event, attempting to understand Christ and his relevance in terms of their contemporary problems

[1] From *The Selected Poems of Archibald Lampman* (Toronto: Ryerson Press, 1947).

228]

and concepts, so in every age the Incarnation at the heart of one's lived faith must provide the key for understanding the infinite meaning of each new problem, situation, and epoch.

THE COVENANTAL STRUCTURE OF NATURE

The enigma of creation is forcing our age to the recognition that the fundamental problem of man is man himself. And from the perspective of the Christian revelation man is seen as a creature in which resides both being and nonbeing, for his essential quality is freedom. The Divine intent for man is freely to affirm God in love and thereby to say "yes" to creation, to affirm the Creator and thereby to become co-partner with him in the destiny of completing creation. Freedom may, indeed, become rebellion in which the incompleteness of creation comes as threat, and yet from the perspective of the Covenant even such threat is seen as preparation for the positive meaning of creation. God has graciously willed that the process of creation be that of a Divine-human venture.

But even more is revealed. The historical Covenant with Israel was a promised relationship for which creation itself was intended. Consequently, the very structure of creation is itself covenantal. It is in the Incarnation that this fact is revealed definitively. In this event the Divine became Incarnated in the human, yet in such a way that human freedom was never violated, but brought to completion. In the Incarnation it is disclosed that the fullness of creation is Divine, that there is a Divine depth in every created thing; it is the Will of God that this depth uniquely in each thing should be realized. God's Will is universal—it is Love. But Love is particular. In every speck of creation is a Divine intent to be realized. Nothing is as it seems to be; all things are as they should be when lighted by the fullness of creation beheld in Jesus Christ.

MAN AS CREATOR

In Jesus Christ is revealed not only the structure of nature, but the vocation for which man was created. In the Incarnation is revealed the *imago Dei* which mankind has rejected but which haunts him continually. This *imago Dei* is the very structure of man which must be fulfilled or his is the frustration which is the "sickness unto death." And who is the God in whose image man is revealed to have been created? The answer is clear—the *Creator* God.

In Jesus Christ, then, the Divine image of the Creator is disclosed in man, and there is revealed the purpose of the Creator, for he has covenanted with man in the creative task. Yet the work of Jesus Christ is not only that of revealing but also of restoring, redeeming. Through the Incarnation God wills forgiveness, ac-

ceptance, whereby man is brought to a new relationship
with God. With the "eyes of faith," one may now in
trust perceive in each new event, each encounter, each
object in all creation, the particular Will of God. For
the man of faith, the distinction between essence and
existence in all things becomes creative. As heir of the
Creator God, illuminated by the Divine-human fulfillment in Jesus Christ, man is restored to the true freedom which, as Paul says, is the beginning of the
transformation of all creation.

> . . . the creation itself will be set free from its bondage
> to decay and obtain the glorious liberty of the children
> of God. We know that the whole creation has been
> groaning in travail together until now; and not only the
> creation, but we ourselves, who have the first fruits of
> the spirit, groan inwardly as we await for adoption as
> sons, the redemption of our bodies. For in this hope we
> were saved. (Romans 8:21-24)

It is this overwhelming vision, emerging from the Incarnation, that we must now consider in some detail.

CALL AND RESPONSE

Freedom is truly freedom only if God remains a
"hidden" God even in his revelation of himself. We
see this in the book of Job. God's eternal wager on
man must be made without man's clear knowledge of
the eternal odds placed upon him. To know with cer-

tainty one's precise task in creation is to become simply
an organ stop in the Divine performance. Unless there
is ambiguity, uncertainty, doubt, alternatives, there
is no freedom and man is no longer a man. The cosmic
process would be no Divine-human partnership, but a
Divine soliloquy.

So in the Incarnation, God is revealed but not un-
deniably; he forgives, but not beyond doubt; he loves,
but not coercively. Man, by the fact of his freedom,
lives by faith, not by sight. Therefore, God's call to
man is neither demand nor requirement, but invitation,
request. To the man restored in Jesus Christ, creation
becomes opened as a creative calling. Expressed theologically, in the lives of those who believe, God in
Christ has promised the gift of his immediate presence.
But man's response to God in love is man's to make,
for while the Holy Spirit is available, it never deprives
freedom, but undergirds and strengthens as it is ap-
propriated.

REDEMPTION AS MEANS, NOT END

But what does the Christian see as, in his new freedom, he responds to the call of God? It is here that
Christendom has wavered between two possibilities.
The one possibility is the ascetic denial of creation,
the personal escape from involvement in life through
an affirmation of complete other-worldliness. The sec-

ond possibility is the creative affirmation of the world
in all its potential and redeemed splendor, the world
of beauty, love, art. This is the vision of a transfigured
creation.

What has kept many Christians from this latter affirmation of the meaning of creation through and for
Incarnation is the thought that the only goal of life is
"salvation." To put it another way, salvation is understood selfishly as an individual rather than a social
and cosmic matter. But redemption from sin, salvation from evil, are in themselves negative. They can
be understood positively only by being seen as preparation for life in the Spirit. Justification or redemption
is only the beginning of the Christian life, not its end.
Redemption is a restoration *for the sake of something,*
or it is meaningless. Negatives can give no positive
meaning to life.

Furthermore, to make "salvation" the goal of life is
to render all history meaningless. That is, if redemption is simply a return of man to his "pre-fallen" state
of naïve innocence, history becomes a circle going no
place. Even if every man were so redeemed, the best
that could be said would be that after one million years
man has reached the state from which he began. All
human activity would be only the attempt of history
to negate itself, to become as though no human act
or Divinely redemptive act had ever been. Redemption is not for its own sake, but for life in the Spirit

wherein one discovers the vision of a transfigured creation.

LIFE IN THE SPIRIT

Since the meaning of creation is revealed through the Incarnation, the Christian has affirmed that all things were created through Christ. The fact that the world is created not by God the Father alone, but, as the creeds insist, by the Father through the Son, is the affirmation of a *continuing* creation. And since freedom is the center of the cosmic purpose, creation begun in the Father, continued through the Son, can be completed only through life in the Spirit. Life in the Spirit is life in creativity. It is the infusion of the Spirit into the spirit of man, and this we call inspiration. All gifts are the Spirit's—not only those of the prophet, the apostle, the saint, but those of the poet, the philosopher, the inventor, and the social reformer as well. The Spirit works in all men, just as the witness of the Father radiates throughout all creation. Despite his will, the nonbeliever is still called to creativity, by a Creator he will not admit, for a work which as it is accomplished stands as a living denial of his understanding of what he is doing. It is only to him who has known the Son that the full and comprehensive meaning of the cosmic task to which he is being called is known.

In one sense, creativity is not a consequence of redemption, but occurs in dialogue with it. Redemption is not immediate, once and for all; it is an unending process. Redemption is negative; creativity is its positive corollary. Together the process is a fulfillment of the new being through the Spirit in relation to creation. Nicolas Berdyaev put his finger on the sin of the Christian in not seeing this: "Christian people desire not so much a real change and transfiguration of their nature as absolution for their sins."

THE FAILURE OF CULTURE

This process which is life in the Spirit involves far more than the transformation of the individual, and it is here that one is feeling for the very heights of the Christian vision. It is the Divine-human call to the transformation of creation. And yet, what can this possibly mean?

It is clear that the history of culture is the history of rise *and* fall, success *and* failure, novelty followed by sterile conformity. A generation ago one might be able to believe in some sort of creative progress, but in our time such talk is idle. We have seen in one generation the devastation of that which has taken centuries to create, not only in the area of material creativity but in the realms of moral, social, and spiritual creativity as well. The problem of human creativity cannot be

solved on the plane of human history, or one must
label it as failure.

The Promise of Resurrection

The problem of human creativity is inevitably thrust
back upon the Christian revelation to see if here an
answer can be found. The response begins as a question: can it be that the God revealed in Jesus Christ
shall say of human creativity in the end, "Truly, I say
to you, there will not be left here one stone upon another, that will not be thrown down"? The God of the
Christian is a refining but not a consuming fire. Man
shall present himself for judgment, but for restoration
as well—"Behold, I make all things new." The final
restoration promised in and through Christ is not the
promise of the immortality of the soul but the resurrection of the body. That is, the promise is not that
some aspect of man will remain after death but that
the *total* man will be restored and brought to perfection. Is there anything more integral to the flesh of
man than the works of his hands? Through the resurrection we are led to believe that the God-given, God-
sustained, God-inspired capacities of creativity will
not be as though they had never been.

Not all the glorious trimmings of a jeweled heaven
could compensate for the total, absolute, and eternal
annihilation of such a work as Bach's *Christmas Ora-*

torio, proffered to God just as it was evoked from man by God. That it stands in sin, yes; that it is less than perfect, yes; that in elevating God, man has sought to elevate himself, yes. But that God will blot it out, forcing man to repent for having brought it forth . . . ? "I call you no longer friends, but sons and heirs of my heavenly Father."

THE KINGDOM OF GOD

It is precisely at this point that the Christian doctrine of the kingdom of God arises in all its relevance. The kingdom of God is the promised consummation of history, the goal of the Divine-human creative venture. For this goal God has revealed himself as in need of man, in need not in the sense that he is not God without man, but in need because he has Willed the Divine-human copartnership. It is in the Incarnation that God has revealed supremely his Will to elevate humanity to the realm of Divine Sonship. This, too, is the meaning of the Ascension. Whatever else it may mean, it is clearly the witness to God's willingness and intent to elevate humanity into his very Being. Such an affirmation as this is as overwhelming as the Christian vision of creativity. Berdyaev expresses it well: "My salvation is bound up with that not only of other men, but also of animals, plants, and every blade of grass—all must be transfigured and brought into the kingdom of God. And this depends upon my creative efforts." Yet as puzzling as these two exhilarating affirmations are, when brought together, they become highly meaningful.

In the Incarnation, revealed in the fullness of its meaning through the Resurrection and Ascension, God has shown his intent to make the creative acts of man part of his own experience. In Jesus Christ, God himself acts, knowing both the sufferings and joys of humanity from within. These he does not cast off in death, but elevates them into himself: humanity is assumed into the inner life of Deity. God has willed that in the depths of our being, our experiences become immediately and intimately part of the experiences of God himself. And, as his experiences, they undergo the interpenetration that provides the meaning-giving thread of continuity to history. Through human creative experience, God has willed to be enriched, so that in the Kingdom yet to be not only will the consciousness of the redeemed man enter but the totality of the Divine-human creative venture as well. Through man's creative acts the Kingdom is coming into being. This Kingdom, however, is not a progressive achievement in history. Rather, through the transforming "memory" of the eternally present God the isolated creative acts within time become constitutive of the Kingdom yet to be. It is God himself who holds together human activity in an ultimate meaning derived from the goal of history, the Kingdom, of which this activity will be constitutive. The Kingdom is not simply a hope but a task, not only a future promise but a present responsibility; it is not the destruction of human history but its completion.

The way of faith is the life of trust in the immediacy of God's providential Will. The creative potentialities in each situation are revealed through the inspiration of the Spirit. Every situation is a new possibility, a fresh beginning, a new calling to a new beauty, a new fulfillment, which has never before been possible. This is the work of man's creative imagination, viewing all things from the perspective of the Divine Fulfillment promised and begun in Jesus Christ. Berdyaev expresses in brilliant fashion this vision of the Kingdom opened by the Christian understanding:

Will there be any sort of positive result of history, or will the result be merely negative? Another way of putting the same question is to ask: Will the creative acts of man . . . enter into the Kingdom of God? . . . The products of great creative minds prepare the way for the Kingdom of God, and enter into it. Greek tragedy, the pictures of Leonardo, Rembrandt, Botticelli; Michelangelo's sculpture and Shakespeare's dramas; the symphonies of Beethoven and the novels of Tolstoy; the philosophical thought of Plato, Kant, and Hegel; the creative suffering of Pascal, Dostoyevsky and Nietzsche; the quest for freedom and for what is

true and right in the life of society—all enter into the
Kingdom of God.[2]

Yet the Christian vision is far more complete than
even this. From the Christian revelation comes the assurance that He who knows the fall of the sparrow
will permit no creation, however seemingly slender,
to fade into nothingness. There is nothing of beauty in
history or in our mundane experiences that He will
not gather unto himself, not simply in judgment, but
in redeemed and transformed fullness. Love is the beginning, middle, and end of creation. And every act
of love, whether in regard to another person, in relation to society, or in the nurturing of nature, whether
it is the creation of beauty in home, business, or field,
all are foretastes as well as instruments in the completion of creation, the attainment of the kingdom of
God. ". . . my chosen shall long enjoy the works of
their hands. They shall not labor in vain . . ." (Isaiah
65:22-23).

CULTURE AS THE EXPRESSION OF ULTIMATE CONCERN

Yet what are we to say from the Christian perspective concerning the meaning of culture in the more
specialized sense—culture as the work of creative

[2] Nicolas Berdyaev, *The Beginning and the End*, trans. R. M.
French (New York: Harper & Brothers, 1952), p. 250. Permission
granted by YMCA-Press, Paris, copyright owners.

genius? Whatever else man is, he is a creator. By his very nature he must act, and to act is to make. And just as man's actions commit him to a wager, conscious or unconscious, concerning ultimate meaning, so the works of a man's hands express profoundly this ultimate concern, this orienting love. Likewise, the corporate works which are culture reflect and express powerfully the faith of an age.

Where, for example, are the most significant achievements in modern architecture? In the Middle Ages, the answer was clear—one need only turn to the cathedrals, overwhelming achievements in architectural prowess, set in the very center of life. Here we see, brilliantly expressed, the faith which permeated the lives of these people. Yet when we turn to the modern period, the change is significant. For the most part, churches are no longer the product of the passion of the Christian spirit wrestling with contemporary building materials to create a living declaration of ultimate concern. Most often, Christian faith has become so sterile that both its people and its architects can only rely on the faith of the past, building New England meeting houses on the plains of Kansas, and pseudo-gothic cathedrals on university campuses of supposedly advanced learning. Where then are the important examples of modern architecture? Quite expectedly, at those points where the faith of modern man centers, in the houses of its objects of worship—business and industry. The Empire State Building stands majestically as the new St. Peter's of twentieth-century America. Whatever else the artist may be, he is certainly a weathercock of his times.

CULTURE AS PROPHETIC WITNESS

In the case of the individual, it is clear that the God which one confesses with his lips is often not the "god" which one serves with his life. And still further, it is the disturbing fact that the individual is not even aware of his "polytheism," or call it hypocrisy, if you will. So is the case with groups, nations, and periods. Self-deception is the creator of the pride which destroys self and group.

It is from this perspective that the prophetic role of culture becomes clear. The real faith, the *lived meaning* of an age as opposed to simply its token assent, is reflected best and exposed most powerfully through the significant art of that age. In literature, painting, architecture, and the like, an age is mirrored to itself so that it can see itself for what it is. It is for this reason that we have used contemporary literature in our study, for therein the most sensitive creators of our time are sensing prophetically the bankruptcy of twentieth-century faith, forcing us to encounter both ourselves and life with ruthless honesty.

And yet the arts are prophetic not only in terms of

the honesty of their reflection. Although the artistic genius is born with a unique sensitivity which reflects powerfully his times, he is honed and edged by the conditions of life around him to the point of agonizing unrest. The true artist is always in the ambivalent position of immersing himself in contemporary life in all its sordid and dismal dimensions, often to the point of sensuality, and yet, as we have seen in contemporary literature, within this near capitulation is to be heard the voice of the artist prophesying *against* the superficiality of his age. The artist moves restlessly through what is, in the agonizing search for the fulfillment of creation, for the beauty that ought to be.

Consequently, it is through culture in general and the arts in particular that come not only powerful portrayals but also dramatic critiques of the contemporary faith according to which men are living.

Culture as Creative Discovery

The mediocre art work is only reflective of a cultural faith-situation, for it is simply the product of that faith. The true work of art, however, is a reflection which is judgment because it is likewise discovery. The great artist does not stop with a portrayal of the contemporary situation, no matter how powerful. Rather, the artist of genius passes inevitably through artistic critique to creative affirmation. He creates in a very real sense of the word. He takes the raw experiences of existence and creates from them a world that is new, and yet, it is not a world formed by his own desires. It is a world that places a claim on us as exhibiting life as it truly is beneath its surface, viewed in terms of the potentialities revealed by the artist's unique vision. Art is created by an honest and unflinching gaze at the world in all its sordidness, undergirded by a vision of its possibilities. The created world of the artist has about it the spirit of "oughtness," for so it comes to the artist, and so it is readdressed to the audience as demand.

From the Christian perspective, artistic creativity emerges from the dialogue between essence and existence, between depth potentiality and present actuality. Art passes beyond imitation of things as they now are, groping for a unity of form and content, for a completion and consummation of the essence-existence tension characterizing reality itself. Art is the revelation of the form inchoate in the raw materials of space and time. In bringing the meaning-giving form of anything to clarity, to incarnate completion, the artist is witnessing to the very structure and meaning of the Divinely intended order in which all things live, move, and have their being.

Great art is judged by its ability to probe so profoundly into one point in time and space that it uncovers the abiding and the universal for all time and all space. *King Lear*, for example, makes a claim upon us not as an ancient King of Britain but as every man caught in the tragedy of his own blind pride. Art completes the concrete which in its fullness radiates with the meaning that is universal.

Art is best defined this way: it is the dramatic expression of felt realities potential to man and nature. Its intent is to search for and expose an organic state of affairs, and by so doing to bring it more fully into being. The artist's task is truth telling, but truth is not restricted to mere fact. His attempt is to reveal what is there and all around us, but which to us in our daily life is not apparent in its most meaningful and revelatory pattern. Art, in the last analysis, is the creation of beauty. Whatever is ugly, ill-formed, is not art, except insofar as it is a portrayal of the presently actual for the sake of its transfiguration.

It is through Christian revelation that the ultimate foundation for this human capacity is seen: creative imagination has as its task that which most perfectly resembles the activity of the Divine Creator himself—bringing being from nonbeing through the freedom, the organic integrity, in the depth of existent things. As God loves man in his freedom, so the artist loves God's creation, not for his own ends but for the creation itself, and in his loving brings creation to symbolic completion as God would have it.

CULTURE AS THE CREATOR OF FAITH

Art, then, not only reveals an age to itself, not only serves as prophet in periods of shallow and dissipated meaning, but also reveals in profound manner the potentialities resident within a situation. In this role art is a creator and rejuvenator of a culture's inner vitality or faith. The Gothic cathedral, for example, was not only an expression of medieval faith, but to an even greater extent, it was the creator of this faith; these two aspects of art function together. Not only did these men express their faith in such work, but by so creating they came to discover the meaning and fuller dimensions of that faith; and those who followed were molded in their ultimate concern far more by such cathedrals than by the theology of Bonaventure and Aquinas combined.

It is very easy for us to discount the importance of art by understanding it to be a very specialized matter, a task for genius and a product for the museum. But this is far from the case. Man's every act is art, for art is any expression of the free human spirit. Most of our expressions may not qualify as good art, but they cannot escape functioning as art. Each of us is engulfed by such expressions in every moment of his existence, nurturing or deadening his sensitivities, calling forth or undercutting his creative awareness of his cosmic vocation.

To use but a minor illustration, psychology has clearly shown the effect of color on not only the quantity but the quality of the work performed in its presence. How much more powerful, then, is the molding effect of the architectural forms in and around which a man works and lives, the city and street pattern through which he moves, the very design of the countless instruments of daily existence down to the silverware with which life is sustained. The "split-level personality" is a phrase that expresses well the relation between artistic forms and the condition of the self.

The fact that we hesitate to call most of this environment "art" is not to minimize the importance of art in creating individual and cultural faith. Rather, our hesitancy must be taken as judgment on a culture such as our own in which contemporary man is being formed by art not worthy of the name, shaped by creative expressions that in their fantastic inferiority are stultifying, perverting man's sensitivity, self-understanding, and goal in, with, and toward life.

If modern man is a hollow creature spewing forth a hollow culture, an ugly creature divorced from beauty, we must see such "art" as more than present judgment. Much of the tragedy of the present is that the new generation coming into being is struggling into existence in the midst of a culture that in every direction is thrusting ugliness and impotence into the very fiber of its being.

The same is true of great art. If the best artistic creators of a period perceive only "sound and fury," we have not only a mirroring of the hollowness of that present but, even more important, the prophecy of the bankruptcy of the near-future, for it is from the emptiness of such "creative" vision that that culture will draw its meaning, vitality, and images. Creative genius strives for wholeness, for the fullness of being which is beauty. Art is the attempt to bring into symbolic actuality the values potential to a situation. In this way creative genius opens its times to the Divine Call to creativity, to the transfiguration of life in beauty. The call to beauty comes through beauty; and beauty is known through initiation, by living daily in its presence. To be closed to beauty, to a creative vision of fullness, is to be denied the central function of the human spirit. Human life is dynamic; if man is deprived of the images of beauty, he will be filled with the "unconscious" images of demonic possibility. Dostoevsky knew this well: "The awful thing is that beauty is mysterious as well as terrible. God and the devil are fighting there and the battlefield is the heart of man." But, he concluded, "Beauty is a great force, and it will save the world."

THE THEOLOGICAL BASIS FOR ART

These reflections on the nature of art have their basis in the Christian understanding of reality. As the Christian finds in the Trinity the nature of the Divine Activity in the world, so the Trinity provides, as we have seen, the foundation for the Divine-human task of creativity. It is in this light that the ultimate nature of art must be understood.

The artist stands as the most perfect expression of the image of the Creator God in every man, and thus of the Divine Call to man. Whether the artist is aware of it or not, the creation of artistic beauty is the "remembrance" of a lost paradise and the yearning for the transfigured Kingdom yet to be. The artist does not create out of nothing, as does God; he continues God's creation by realizing in matter the special Divine Will for things, bringing them toward completion by incarnating their forms in the flesh of the world. The artist does not copy God's creation but finishes it, releasing its potential beauty. Through the inspiration of the Holy Spirit, the Divine depths within both self and nature are united so that the forms of things yearning for completion, for incarnate wholeness, are discovered and brought to fulfillment.

Art, then, is an anticipation of a completion that nature itself cannot perfectly attain on the finite level, but only at the end of time. And yet it is a foretaste that contributes to the cosmic transfiguration to be. Whether the artist is aware of it or not, art and the creative vocation are witnesses to the Trinitarian structure of reality itself, created and sustained by and in the very Nature and Will of God. In the originating idea in the mind of the artist is the human counterpart of the Father in his creation from nothing. This idea is incarnated in the material of the art work as the Father's intention for the cosmos took on revealing flesh in space and time. The incarnated idea communicates in power through one's experience in its presence as the Father through the Son in the Holy Spirit pervades man and nature that all may participate in transfiguration. Father, Son, Holy Spirit—idea, form, power—artist, art work, audience—the Creator God and the creator man: like illuminates like. Even the pattern of creation, fall, and the redemption finds its counterpart in the purity of the artistic vision, wrestling with the chaotic condition of materials of this world, attempting to find the wedding of form and content with the illuminating power to restore the participant to his proper relation with all creation.

THE DIVINE CALL TO CULTURE

Man, by birth, enters a culture, and this culture is Divinely intended: God has called man to culture. By God's Will, culture is the call to create new beauty never before seen or known. The special Divine Will for each aspect of creation is revealed in each new present by the Holy Spirit, through that creative dialogue of essence and existence perfectly realized in the Incarnation. As Paul said, "God has revealed to us through the Spirit. For the Spirit searches everything, even the depths of God." (I Corinthians 2:10) Art is the finite "model" for the Divine Call to man for the recreation and transfiguration of all things in beauty. A culture that is simply the copy of the past or only an idle repetition of its own self not only exhibits the shallowness of that generation's lived faith, but declares as well the bankruptcy of its creative call and response to all life. An analysis of the significant art of an age reveals the depth of that epoch's "understanding" of its total Divine-human creative vocation as well as the power of its images to evoke such creativity. In this sense art is truly prophetic, for in it is the portrayal of the depth of creative apprehension achieved by the gifted of an age, the vision from which that generation and the one to come does and will draw both its calling and its substance.

* * *

Here, then, is a Christian understanding of Creation from the perspective of the Incarnation. It is one of the most significant aspects of our generation that although, on the one hand, the enigma of creation has forced with new seriousness the religious question, on the other hand, it is from the unique creative possibilities of this desperate situation that the fullness of the Christian world-view for all life may again be recognized and explored in depth. In this Christian understanding of creativity resides a faith with cosmic implications which can transform every aspect of human life. Not simply is it the hope that there will be an eventual meaning. Rather, it is a faith which makes a *sacrament* of every human act, instilling every moment and every situation with infinite possibility, infinite challenge, infinite meaning. It is through the creative imagination in every man that God the Holy Spirit gives man the unfathomable grace to create with him.

Love is the motive for existence and action; beauty is its goal and completion. In their perfection together, neither are self-centered—love comes into being in order to give; beauty is created in order to be shared. Love is the yearning for the completion of all things; beauty is its realization. Creation is through love for love; love is through Creation for Incarnation; and Incarnation is through love for transfiguration. In the words of Paul, the whole creation groaneth and travaileth in pain together until now, waiting with eager longing to be set free from its bondage to decay. In Jesus Christ, "God reconciled the world to himself," that through the Holy Spirit all things may come to the measure of the stature of the fullness of Christ, putting off the old nature and putting on the new. That toward which we are called in and through our freedom in Christ is the new creation, which is his body, "the fullness of him who fills all in all." This we know, "for he has made known to us in all wisdom and insight the mystery of his will, according to his purpose which he set forth in Christ as a plan for the fullness of time, to unite all things in him, things in heaven and things on earth" (Ephesians 1:9-10).

The creative genius testifies by his work to these things, even though he may do so unknowingly, following blindly a transcendent call in ignorance of who calls and for what. Yet this same capacity for creativity resides in its own way in each of us, and it is the basis for our total activities. Man by nature is creator, and in his Divinely intended craving to create he will either elevate himself to self-defeating divinity, or serve in loving response the God of Creation who calls him to copartnership.

It is for the Christian, who knows the joy of the Divine promise of Incarnation fulfilled in Resurrection, that this creative call has full meaning. It comes from One who has summoned man as his co-creator, through him who makes all things new. In the Incarnation, we know the God who is united with us in suffering, taking upon himself the sins and agonies of man. In the Resurrection and Ascension we know the God who

has reclaimed that which he has shared—himself, but
who has also taken to himself that which he has assumed—humanity. It was the *God-man* who ascended
into Heaven. It is he who takes up within himself, who
restores, purifies, and brings to perfect beauty, the
works of our hands. "I will seek that which was lost,
and bring again that which was driven away, and will
bind up that which was broken, and will strengthen
that which was sick." He who can bring good out of
all things will mold into the very fabric of his Kingdom that which we through him are bringing into being. Those with only the mentality to lift the head
of a fallen flower are not to be forgotten, for in such
an act the meaning of all creation is present.

*Lord, I know not what to ask of Thee. Thou only
knowest what I need. Thou lovest me better than I
know how to love myself. Father, give to Thy child
that which he himself knows not how to ask. Smite or
heal, depress me or raise me up; I adore all Thy purposes without knowing them. I am silent; I offer myself
up in a sacrifice; I yield myself to Thee; I would have
no other desire than to accomplish Thy Will. Teach me
to pray. Pray Thyself in me.*

—François Fenelon (1651-1715)

HADDAM HOUSE is an editorial venture in the area of religious literature, which has grown out of the common concerns of The Edward W. Hazen Foundation, the Young Men's Christian Association, and the Young Women's Christian Association. It is interested primarily in the moral and religious questions of students and other young people, although many of its books appeal to a wider audience, including the leaders and teachers of youth.

Through an Editorial Advisory Committee HADDAM HOUSE studies the changing needs for religious literature, plans books, and seeks as authors not only experienced writers but also new voices qualified to give fresh guidance to young men and women in these days. The present membership of the Editorial Advisory Committee includes: Richard T. Baker, *Chairman*, Wayne Cowan, *Secretary*, A. Graham Baldwin, David Byers, Virginia Corwin, John D. Maguire, John O. Nelson, James Rietmulder, Roger L. Shinn, Jean M. Whittet, and Winnifred Wygal.

See the following page for a complete list of HADDAM HOUSE books currently available.

HADDAM HOUSE BOOKS